PRAISE FOR NAVIGATING BEYOND CRISIS

«Ranging from communication, cultural resilience, approaches to resources and confident decision-making, Thomas Lahnthaler aims to demystify the term crisis to help planners to stop underestimating themselves and to encourage us to think differently about preparing to deal with crises. Drawing upon Lahnthaler's extensive personal experience in managing crises, this book is an engaging, thought provoking and intelligent read.»
– Emily Hough, Editor in Chief, The Crisis Response Journal & Director of Crisis Management Ltd.

«As our world is seemingly devastated by more global crises of increasing magnitude, this timely book brings hope. Packed with both captivating stories and practical strategies for crises management, Thomas Lahnthaler delivers much needed, human centric advice on the subject. Navigating Beyond Crisis is a terrific tool for both individuals and businesses to drawn upon.»
–Dennis Geelen, Author of The Zero In Formula

«Insightful and a point of inspiration! Thomas Lahnthaler breaks down very complex crisis issues into a practical framework that can be understood by all. He gives a unique perspective that cultivates a behaviour of better understanding and handling of complex crisis issues.»
– Elona Krypta, Global Expert in Development Finance in Emerging Markets

«This book builds on a wealth of personal experiences, challenging the reader to rethink how to approach crisis management. It showcases the importance of understanding oneself, those around us and the context that we find ourselves in during a crisis. This work represents a great resource for those looking to work in crisis management as well as those already in the field.»
– Regis Chapman, Country Director at World Food Programme

«Thomas finds a beautiful way to showcase elements of crisis management through his personal stories. These lessons can be easily applied equally to personal and professional settings. A must-read for anyone looking to discover techniques on how to become more resilient.»
– Julia Stefani, Director of Product Management - Crypto, SoFi

NAVIGATING BEYOND CRISIS

Thomas Lahnthaler

CONTENT

DEDICATION 8

FOREWORD 10

INTRODUCTION 12

PART I: FUNDAMENTALS.....................17

#1 FOCUS ON PEOPLE 19

#2 CONSIDER HOW TO FRAME COMMUNICATION....35

PART II: CRAFT.......................................61

#1 BUILD A FOUNDATION FOR REINVENTION 63

#2 DEEP-DIVE INTO RESOURCES 75

#3 PRACTICE HABITUAL READINESS 87

PART III: APPLICATION......................105

#1 PROFILE THE CRISIS SYSTEM 107

#2 EXPAND YOUR OPTIONS..................125

#3 MAKE CONFIDENT DECISIONS 139

THE AFTERMATH 151

FINAL THOUGHTS 155

TOOLBOX...158

DECISION NAVIGATOR 164

DEDICATION

It's time to show my appreciation for the people without whom this book would never have been possible.

My family

Thank you for enduring the ups and downs with me on this adventure. You were nothing but supportive, understanding, encouraging, and loving throughout this process, which was marked with enthusiasm, mental absence, frustrations, spontaneous creative spells, and endless notes everywhere around the house. You continue to be the source of my inspiration and backbone. With all my love.

Anisa

You have had an endless number of roles throughout this journey: coach, psychiatrist, teacher, motivator, critic, reality checker, and the list goes on. Most of all, you have a gift that you have applied tirelessly since the outset. You are one of a few people who can translate my often-chaotic thoughts into something that everyone understands. There would be no book without you. Thank you.

Colin, Wolf, Steffi, Maxwell

Your creative skills and support mean a lot to me. You provided the beautiful illustrations, the exciting cover, and the linguistic polish that turned the manuscript into an actual book. I appreciate your dedication to making this the best version of itself.

Friends & Network

I have received support and encouragement beyond anything that I could have ever dreamed of. At many steps along the way, your support made me take the next step, and I'm eternally grateful for that. And while there are too many parties to mention, I hope you know who you are.

Colleagues

I have had the pleasure to work with incredibly dedicated and passionate colleagues. Thank you for bearing with me; trusting me in leading you; and allowing me to try, fail, and learn. Without you, I wouldn't have been able to manage many of these challenging situations.

My Invisible Teachers

In context of being tormented by crises and suffering, you came into my life and proved the most inspiring, courageous, strong, and resilient individuals I have ever met. I am eternally humbled and grateful that you have allowed me to listen to your wisdom, observe your endurance, and learn from your ways to navigate crises. Your faces are with me, and this book is dedicated to you.

FOREWORD

"Do not ever assume you know how you will react in a crisis."

– Thomas Lahnthaler

In the last two years, encircled by walls between loss, loneliness and forced levity, we were pushed to rebuild our identity. The world drew simultaneously closer and distant testing systems, shifting bonds and revealing deep connections in profound encounters. I was born and raised in a country held hostage by uncertainty. And I have had the privilege of working with people and communities in crisis for most of my life. Yet it wasn't until I walked out of the clinic where I was based and into eerily deserted London streets that first night of lockdown in March 2020 when I fully stopped to think deeply about crisis. Months later, Thomas would pose the question what we would call it if we didn't call it crisis at all, the complex simplicity of which can only arise from those who have stared it in the face. And stare it he has. Living and leading through crisis in nearly two decades and 30 countries. With lessons from direct raw connections and deep introspections by someone who sat down to write because he had stood up to live. And who in Navigating Beyond Crisis with the contrast, piercing observations and gentleness that characterise him has written as much a work of philosophy as an important practical text for all sectors rooted in vulnerability and storytelling. An approach to crisis management and life that has at its core the one thing that matters most, people. A book that guides without dictating. One that poses questions without asking them and provides answers through the only certainty that rests in continuously battling assumptions. A book built with the flexibility to sail at leisure or navigate at high speed as required by need and circumstance. The kind of writing and self-reflection only made possible by blending critical thinking with deep sensitivity, skill, gritty experience, and honest expression. A space where opportunities come with a door handle. I once read that we write to taste life twice, in the moment and in retrospect. Perhaps we live it that way too. As you do, I hope you reach for this book to help illuminate and anchor your journey whether facing alleyways you've marked and left behind or starring at the winding roads to come.

Anisa Goshi
London, 2022

INTRODUCTION

It's hard to pinpoint when the journey of writing this book started – when I happened to be around New York City on 9/11, during my final paper while researching atrocities and human rights violations against the Pygmy population in Ituri in the Eastern Democratic Republic of Congo, when I was offered my first volunteer job and travelled to rural South Africa, when I was carrying out my first humanitarian field training, or somewhere in between. As I look back on being a humanitarian worker for the past fifteen years, I'm grateful for the privilege of having worked in thirty countries, many of which have been marked by long-lasting conflicts and devastating crises, and I can see the inspiration for this book in all of them. But you see, I never considered myself a writer. My teachers might even say I was more of a talker. Yet, writing a book was always one of those secret dreams of mine – one of those "one-day" dreams that you know have a slim chance of coming true, though as it turns out slim isn't none, despite the writer's arduous workload. When COVID-19 conquered the world and captured the headlines as a global pandemic, I was frequently asked for advice by people and companies given my background in managing and dealing with large-scale humanitarian crises. At that time, I had taken a hiatus from crisis management, but the situation served as a spark that would ultimately reignite my interest in and return to the field. Stranded on a peninsula, surrounded by a forest, and wholly secluded, I had a lot of time to reflect on what I would advise with respect to working on such a complex large-scale crisis that cut across all sectors and aspects of life. Then, one evening around Christmas 2019, triggered by a documentary about Bangladesh where I had been among the first to respond to the situation of Rohingya refugees fleeing Myanmar two years earlier, I wrote an article about my experiences and some of the dilemmas I faced during my career as a humanitarian. Diving into these memories was like opening Pandora's box, and the stories kept coming, seemingly having waited to be discovered all this time. The article wasn't linguistically mind-blowing, but the content resonated with people and was well-received by readers. However, despite the positive feedback, it took a lot more encouragement by very determined friends and family members to continue writing, (and a whole lot more to share it publicly), but without realising or planning, first came a few articles, followed by the first chapters and late nights of inspiration. Next came endless revisions and frustration, endless impatience, too much to say and no idea how to get it out, more encouragement, reminders to embrace the process when writer's block and the realities of daily life would take hold, newfound determination, and finally the light of the finish line. All of this turned into the pages that lie before you now.

SO, WHAT IS THIS BOOK?

I should probably start by what it is not.

It's neither a memoir nor an autobiography, though it contains episodes from my life connected to the reflections that follow them.

It's not a how-to book, though there are elements that can be interpreted as advice and practical steps.

It's not a general guideline to crisis management, though it contains relevant guidance. It's also not an academic book, though I reference some models and insights that have helped me frame my thoughts and practice.

Finally, it is not meant as a criticism or for exposure, which is why I refrain from naming organisations or work locations. I am grateful to each of them for giving me the opportunity to follow my purpose and learn while under their banner. Without these opportunities and trust in my abilities, none of the stories or insights in this book would have been possible.

WHAT IS IT THEN?

This is entirely up to you, the reader. The following pages contain a collection of ideas and insights in a structure that outlines my mindset and approach to dealing with crises. For me, it was a way to understand, frame, and share what I have learned over the years. The result is a mix of practical elements, reflections, learnings, and thoughts for further exploration. I do not claim this way is the only way or the most effective, but it is *my* way. Some of the elements might fall contrary to what colleagues and other experts in the field offer, argue, and suggest. This is by no means intended to contradict or diminish them, and it is, in fact, thanks to their work that I realised and concluded the approach that works better for me. Of course, I would be very happy if you take something from it and find a thing or two that proves useful in your work or personal life. This choice I leave for you to make.

HOW TO USE THIS BOOK

The book is structured in three parts: Fundamentals, Craft, and Application. You can read the book from beginning to the end, which is what I would recommend, or if a specific topic is appealing to you, you can read the respective chapter on its own. There are minor references to other chapters across the book, but I felt it important to provide a flexible model, where you can read about what you feel is most relevant without losing an overall essence of understanding. There are practical exercises that include steps regarding their application, but do bear in mind that these steps are no more than suggestions, and like every exercise or process, I recommend finding your own way.

This book might be of interest to you if you currently work or have worked with crises actively, are planning to do so imminently or in the future, or you are faced with a crisis professionally or privately. Navigating turbulent, uncertain times is something we all must face at one point or another, and I hope you find a new idea, perspective, or point of inspiration ahead. If I help you dare to reinvent when the going gets tough, I'll have surely succeeded.

Lastly, I do not take for granted that you are reading this book, and I want to express my appreciation and gratitude. I hope you find the following pages as enjoyable, useful, insightful, and thought-provoking as I found the process of writing them.

Thomas Lahnthaler

PART I
FUNDAMENTALS

#1 FOCUS ON PEOPLE

We had been on the road for two hours, and the impressions around me started to merge into one incomprehensible image of devastation. The fact that I had just driven along one of the longest sandy beaches in the world became an insignificant footnote. I had never seen so many people in need at once, yet I knew I wasn't even looking at a fraction of those who had settled on these seemingly endless hills of mud in the south of Bangladesh. It was overwhelming and impossible to process all of my reactions as we continued the trip. There were tens of thousands of men and women – including senior citizens, people with disabilities, and children, the suffering of whom hit me even harder, deeper, and more painfully, as I had recently become a father. When we finally arrived at our destination, my team was already waiting exhausted and mirroring a lot of the emotions that I had experienced on the way. We were there to deal with the crisis, the context, and the situation, but looking around me, it became clear there was something else that needed our focus: people.

EVERYTHING STARTS AND ENDS WITH US

Over many years of managing crises around the world, I looked upon them as situations that needed managing, in alignment with most definitions about crisis management, which highlight the handling of unexcepted events. Reflecting on this definition later, I questioned whether we would talk about a crisis if there were no people affected, and I don't think so. Though I'm not arguing there are no crises outside the human sphere, it still takes people to label and manage them as such. Crises are a human phenomenon. Thus, crisis management is always human-centric.

Self-care and self-reflection are key for making it through a crisis, and there is nothing selfish about this. It starts with acceptance and the will to take an honest look in the mirror at any time, acknowledging our physical, mental, and emotional state. These must be determining factors for whether we are suited to be involved in managing a crisis. Our many inner voices constantly represent our fears, values, worries, emotions, needs and desires. Distinguishing these voices is difficult, as they come with overwhelming messages that we might not feel is the right time to assess and consider during a critical situation. Consequently, we often choose to ignore them instead of working with them. They may not all be equally relevant, but some give us indications for how we are doing at all levels, so it's vital to take the time to identify and listen to them all.

What initially made me avoid these reflections was apprehension about what I might uncover – namely, feelings of pressure, insecurity, uncertainty, and even fear, which I thought might compromise my ability to manage or be involved in managing a crisis. I was also overly concerned that I would be considered unsuitable for the work by my colleagues and managers. This was false pride and a misplaced sense of responsibility. If I'm not capable of being involved in managing a crisis because it triggers me or I have private things to deal with and might be distracted, it's more responsible to step away than stick it out. Being at 50 per cent of my potential might make the work for all involved more difficult and negatively impact team morale. It can be a dilemma, but it's important to know yourself, and there is nothing wrong with saying no. We all have to step away sometimes.

When involved in crisis management, once the situation starts to calm down, it is essential that we take a break to reflect on and learn from our actions and reactions. It is necessary to honestly assess how we felt and behaved in the situation and get a better picture of ourselves. Knowing our own capabilities and limitations is a core element in effectively managing a crisis and the people involved in it. The same applies when we deal with different and ever-changing contexts. Situations can be overwhelming, and it is important to acknowledge this is the case, find space to pause, and regularly take an honest look inwards. It is also helpful to get perspectives on how people perceive you from the outside. This gives you an insight into whether there is a mismatch between your self-perception and your actual state of wellbeing.

Lastly but no less critically, remember you are as much affected by the crisis that you are managing as everyone around you. Every time I am faced with a crisis, I try to remind myself of the looks that surrounded me in myriad different situations. Those eyes who have investigated mine are great reminders that to successfully manage a critical situation, you must learn how to manage human multitudes first and focus on people before anything else. So, how can this be done?

ALIGN PERCEPTIONS

Our realities are constructs of our differing perceptions. I first became aware of this in my work as a conflict mediator. Initially, it's difficult to comprehend how conflict parties are unable to see their common ground, which I can clearly observe from my role and position. Often, they disagree for the very same reasons. Yet, they see the situation from their perspective only, rooted in their perceptions and reinforced by their need to maintain their individual autonomy. The divide makes it difficult for them to see the bigger picture, including plentiful commonalities. For most conflict parties, resolving the conflict isn't automatically about clear, logical solutions. It's first and foremost about being humans with feelings and the need for their individual realities to be acknowledged. Only then can they start to align them to a common reality.

The same applies to crises. They, too, are constructs, fed by the system (and the narrative spun around it) as much as our perceptions. The term itself doesn't offer a clear description or explanation of what a particular crisis is; we use it to describe the situation, but our perspectives and interpretations differ, influenced by our previous experiences. To illustrate the fact that we talk about the same things with different meanings, answer this question with the first word that comes to mind without overthinking it: *What is the opposite of a crisis and what makes this the opposite for you?*

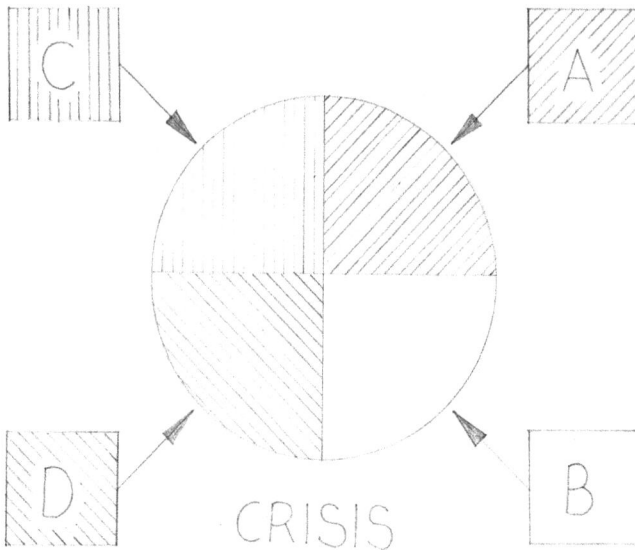

Figure 1 – Crisis Construction

When I conduct this exercise in group settings, responses often include words such as stability, safety, security, and some might even answer boredom or stagnation. In any case, the answers differ, and even if the chosen opposites align, the interpretation may not. The hidden usefulness of this exercise is in giving an indication of what we are striving towards in a crisis allowing us to get an understanding of our feelings and what we are missing. These emotional reactions feed into our perception of the term and influence our response to it. They further reveal what we will subconsciously work towards when dealing with a critical situation, regardless of whether it's as individuals or as part of a team.

Therefore, as a first step, it's important to create a common understanding and expand your image of the crisis among the people you are surrounded by or who work with you. Keep in mind this is not an exercise about being right or wrong but about sharing and growing the understanding of a crisis to expand options for getting through it. Furthermore, by creating a common understanding, we can also ensure that we work in the same direction instead of subconsciously pursuing our own goals. This helps align and increase resources and their use. So, next time, take a moment and ask yourself this: *Are we all talking about the same crisis?*

DEALING WITH HUMAN DYNAMICS

As part of my work, I have had the privilege of being allowed to learn from Indigenous peoples. They have generously shared parts of their knowledge and ancient wisdom with me, which I try to appropriately honour and transfer into my approach and our modern way of living. One of the key elements that all Indigenous communities have in common is interconnectedness and the understanding that humans are simply a part of something bigger – that each of us must play a role for everything to work. Nevertheless, working and living closely also means being able to handle the side-effects of basic human dynamics. A volatile and dynamic context triggers insecurity in us and emotional reactions intensify the occurrence of human dynamics. Crises are accompanied by stress, disruption, changes in processes, and changes in communication. The tone gets rougher, the structures more hierarchical, and the messages more direct. Isolated, each element would already be challenging for a team to absorb, so imagine dealing with them all at once.

Human dynamics aren't a one-off. They follow the development of the fast-changing context and the subsequent impact it has on our situation. It's essential to establish processes that deal with these dynamics and create an open and transparent way of handling them. Ideally, these norms are established early in the crisis and revisited regularly. If managed effectively, human dynamics are an intense driving force for innovative ways to deal with critical situations. The exchange of different approaches helps to deconstruct assumptions and identify potential blind spots. Furthermore, dynamic co-creation of solutions from a diverse group of people is an extremely effective way of expanding your options and choices for how to deal with a situation. They are also very important when it comes to ensuring high motivation and engagement – and similarly effective when working through down periods, which are common during a crisis.

WORKING WITH EMOTIONS

A friend I had lived with in Afghanistan came to visit when I was stationed in Rome. Culturally, our neighbourhood was very strongly connected to supporting one of the two main Roman football clubs, and whenever their team was playing at home, they would throw firecrackers in their backyards, exploding between buildings and houses. It was extremely noisy. My friend wasn't used to this situation, and his only reference point was the explosions we had experienced in Afghanistan. In reaction to post-traumatic stress, he became increasingly agitated and angry and would run to the balcony, shouting at the boys to throw their crackers somewhere else, a response that might seem disproportional to many, yet one to which I can very much relate. To this day, I hold no appreciation for fireworks of any kind. While this is a rather extreme example, the analogy illustrates the challenge presented to us by crises; they naturally trigger strong emotional reactions. I have witnessed repeatedly how simply hearing the term without context can trigger memories, mental images, and consequently emotions.

Emotions signal that certain situations, words, smells, or sounds move something within us – the initial and uncontrolled response from our body and mind telling us what is happening on the inside. Emotions aren't yet categorised feelings, and trying to control them is difficult. They come unexpected and differ in intensity. We might be able to control our impulses and how we show them, however, we must not also try to suppress our emotions. Suppressing emotions deprives us of the possibility to work with them and explore their origin, which would allow us to know ourselves better. It robs us of the chance to discover our doubts, what makes us feel threatened, and other elements to which we or our team members react subconsciously in a crisis.

Claiming we can ignore emotions and decide rationally in crisis management is unwise and will potentially make managing the crisis more challenging. I have been part of teams where managers dismissed emotions, arguing that it was essential to keep a cool head and decide rationally. As a result, we all buried our emotions and were afraid to talk about them openly. Nevertheless, we couldn't stop them from resurfacing with even higher intensity and at the most inconvenient of times. In addition, the accumulated mix of pent-up emotions made it more difficult to handle them and work with them positively. My encouragement to any sceptical leader who might argue they don't have time for emotions in a crisis is to consider whether they want to spend a little time dealing with this important aspect early on or a considerably greater deal of time at an unknown and unpredictable point during the crisis. In my experience, those who knowingly or unknowingly opted for the second scenario regretted it. Keeping emotions in the forefront of your mind and handling them as they surface will place you at an advantage and in a much better situation.

I must also bust the myth that emotions are bad for decision-making in crisis. I have experienced the opposite to be true, provided we know how to work with them. Emotions, as mentioned above, function as our inner compass. They reveal information that we have not yet decoded, of which we cannot always make sense, and whose intensity is often scary. However, once we embark on exploring our emotions, interesting things start to emerge. Not only does the intensity decrease, but we also get to the core of our reactions and what triggers them. Anger, for example, is a very special and intense reaction, which I refer to as an umbrella emotion that blocks access to emotions brewing underneath it. Anger generally isn't advised as a good state of mind in which to make decisions. However, it's important to give it space, and if channelled effectively, anger can be a driver for finding alternative solutions to problems, as it provides a strong focus and a high level of energy. If not dealt with, as is the case with any other emotion, anger will return and might grow into fury, rage, or withdrawal, becoming even more difficult to handle.

Our decision-making also becomes a lot more focused when we are under stress and have emotional responses. The most prominent example of this is instinctive decisions, such as squatting when we hear a loud bang, but the same is true for less instinctive ones. Sometimes when under stress, our brain pre-selects options and leaves us only with what our subconscious assessed as the most feasible ones, thereby significantly shortening the decision-making processes. Neuroscientist Tali Sharot at University College London explains that when experiencing stressful events, whether personal or public, a physiological change is triggered that can cause the brain to become fixated on what might go wrong. She points out it is important to realise that stress travels rapidly from one person to the next. If your co-worker is stressed, you are more likely to tense up and feel stressed yourself. Our brains are designed to transmit emotions quickly to one another because they often convey important information. In situations that are already complex, this can cause a domino effect, so making space for and dealing with emotions constantly is key.

RIDE THE ROLLERCOASTER
OF LONG-TERM ENDURANCE

The dynamics that evolve with crises and their impact on us are unpredictable and change frequently. In such situations, there are plenty of moments when difficult decisions need to be made. Each of them comes with enormous pressure and their consequences only crystalise once decisions are implemented. The result isn't always what we hope for, which can lead to frustration, disappointment, and the loss of motivation. This is a natural process that repeats itself in every crisis and is more intense the longer they last. There might be moments when we see the figurative light at the end of the tunnel during a crisis only for the context to change and leave us with the feeling of having moved back to square one, as has been the case with COVID-19. Dynamics like these have a severe impact on our perseverance and endurance. Crisis management involves navigating uncertainty and requires a mindset that allows for disappointing decisions to become opportunities to learn.

In combination with the aforementioned aspects of managing people, endurance is an often-overlooked necessity. Endurance doesn't mean that we must always stand unbent amidst a storm. Rather, it's about finding ways that help us manage the challenges ahead for as long as we can and are mentally able to do so. Endurance is also often mistaken or conflated with having to keep going all the time without stopping. I find this a dangerous misconception – and one to which I have fallen victim. The reality is that we're not able to work around the clock for a long period of time and maintain high performance. In attempting to do so, we merely weaken our endurance, which has a physical, mental, and emotional layer, though they don't have to always be on the same performance level. There are practical, underestimated actions we can take to boost our endurance and positively influence motivation during a crisis to impact all three levels. The five habits that I use when managing longer-term crises to address and work against fatigue are provided below.

Habit 1: Voice frustrations openly

At times, frustration can be overwhelming and start to influence our focus and performance. Sometimes it helps to take short breaks, during which everyone focuses on releasing frustrations in an unfiltered manner. This habit requires a strong ability to handle negative emotions. It's about taking the pressure off and avoiding those irritations that have a lasting effect on motivation. The premise of voicing frustrations needs to be formulated as our individual perspective without any personal attacks and must include a strong consideration of cultural boundaries and sensitivities. An interesting phenomenon that often happens in these sessions is that someone will eventually start to laugh, at which point the negativity and tension transform into a connecting experience. Once the biggest frustrations are out, there is a noticeable positive difference that allows all parties involved to refocus.

Habit 2: Celebrate successes and failures

I often hear that in crises, there's no time for anything. My experience has taught me that there's plenty of time for plenty of things, and one of those things is the celebration of successes – and failures. If the focus is on work only and successes are never acknowledged, it will impact long-term motivation. Unavoidable setbacks will have a greater negative impact, making it increasingly difficult to recover after each of them. Celebrating successes, however, is more than a simple matter of stating what was achieved. It requires an emotional connection of some kind; otherwise, they turn into mere statements. Failures can and should also be celebrated, followed by reframing them into insights and learnings.

Habit 3: Remember the person behind the function

Nobody is a crisis manager 24/7. We're all people beyond our roles, and it's important to make space for that side of us. In crises, it's easy to forget that there are other considerations beyond the crisis. However, it's dangerous to do so because the world doesn't stop existing simply because we're dealing with a complex issue. In addition, not everyone will be able to relate to the crisis we're busy managing. This, however, is a bias, as the opposite is true for the people not affected by it. Therefore, it's crucial to make dedicated space to talk and remember that people deal with things outside the crisis as well.

Habit 4: Force breaks

Once we are in crisis management mode, we tend to go on autopilot and get lost in solving problem after problem. It can be riding an unhealthy wave because in that moment it might seem like we have unlimited resources, but the crash landing can be very hard afterwards. When we are in an almost manic state of dealing with a critical situation, we need to force ourselves to break. This can initially be done in a structured way to establish the habit. Taking breaks does not only recharge our batteries, but it gives us the chance to take our mind off the problem, thereby challenging inside-the-box syndrome. I found many unexpected creative solutions during and through breaks.

Habit 5: Allow for humour

Crises are serious because of their serious consequences. But who is to say that humour doesn't have a place in managing a critical situation? I've frequently observed that we have the habit of not allowing ourselves to laugh while we manage critical situations. I work very differently and have only made positive experiences with it. Humour is a catalyst for motivation, engagement, and ownership. Laughter also connects. And all of these are key resources in a crisis. There is a fine line between cynicism and humour, but the latter can have an extremely positive impact on morale and the motivation to tackle challenges creatively.

The impressions from my days in Bangladesh still follow me. It was neither the first nor the last crisis where I had seen people suffer, but it was the one that got through my walls of defence. My work there wasn't marked by working with people only, but it was all for and about people, and it's easy to forget that this is where it starts and ends. Whether it's me, my team, or the people affected by it, no matter the crisis, at the end of it all, there are always human lives affected. Being a good crisis manager means never losing focus of the people involved, whether they're presently invisible, surrounding you, or standing in the mirror.

KEY TAKE-AWAYS

▶ Crisis management requires constantly learning about yourself, including your triggers, your competencies, your limitations, and your emotions.

▶ Regularly check your mental, physical, and emotional state, and if needed, step away from managing the situation. This is a sign of maturity and strength rather than weakness and shame.

▶ Suppressing emotions deprives you of a chance to explore them and possibly find hidden solutions in the reason for the emotional reaction. They are an inner compass that gives everyone information about their wellbeing, and they will resurface if they aren't worked through.

▶ Emotions aren't by default bad for decision-making in a crisis. They can be used to your advantage when making decisions if you explore and work with them.

▶ Crisis management requires a mindset of permanent learning. The most important learning from a crisis is found in what worked well. However, it's important that both successes and failures are being celebrated as learning opportunities.

▶ It's important to remember that the person behind every function needs recognition, space, acknowledgement, and the ability to step out of the role.

▶ Humour is a crucial catalyst for success even in crisis situations.

#2 CONSIDER HOW
TO FRAME COMMUNICATION

It was way past midnight. Around me was an Indigenous community in the middle of what's left of the second-oldest rainforest on this planet on the island of Borneo. I had been their guest of honour for the past two days, and they were hosting me in one of their traditional longhouses. They shared food and their strong homemade moonshine with me. They told me about their struggle to prove ownership of what used to be their ancestral land for hundreds of years and how logging companies continued their destruction, while they tried to secure the necessary documentation. It was my first visit, and I already knew it would also be my last. I was there to tell them that because of a political decision, my employer could no longer contribute financially to their struggle. They constantly filled my cup with moonshine, and I worked hard to keep a clear head to communicate what I had come to tell them. There are no words to describe how I felt having to tell these wonderful people whose only goal was to protect their land and livelihoods that they would be alone once again in a fight they had no chance of winning. I was infuriated, devastated, and felt deeply ashamed. All I ever learned about communication felt meaningless – and certain to fail me in that moment. I knew it was down to pure honesty. After I had shared the information and tried to carefully convey the message without creating any false hope, many of them hugged me, others laughed, and some cried. I thought they had misunderstood, and I sought reassurance through my interpreter who simply said: "They smile because they are so incredibly grateful that you didn't lie and for all the support they have received so far. They already knew you weren't going to be around forever. They cry because they are worried about their future. And they laugh because they think you like their moonshine very much."

REFRAMING THE SITUATION

Communication isn't easy, and it becomes even more difficult in challenging contexts, one of which is a crisis. Factors such as insecurity and the unpredictability of the dynamic context make it difficult to find the best message to convey to your audience and reach as many people as possible through it. It is important to acknowledge these limitations and tailor your communication around them. I don't like the term crisis communication and prefer talking about communication in a crisis, as this also covers messaging within a crisis context while not about the crisis itself. Here, I share my experience, methods, and tools for making the process and experience more manageable and impactful.

The framing effect, simplified, is a way to create a cognitive bias towards reality by establishing a specific frame. This can happen on an individual or collective level and is consistently applied in fields that link to social dynamics and communication. An example of a different frame for the same situation would be to talk about conflict as a chance. To highlight the power of reframing, at The Crisis Compass, we tested the hypothesis that how you communicate in and about a critical situation has an understated impact on how your organisation deals with a crisis. We experimented with splitting ten participants into two groups of five and gave them the same task; having received similar briefs from a fictional CEO, they were asked to write a statement to shareholders under time pressure. Group A received a memo with a focus on crisis and danger while the memo to Group B was focused on opportunity and trust. Both were based on the same exact scenario and facts, but the fundamental differences in response were striking.

After merging the groups together again, they read the statements to each other and followed with a discussion, at which point it became obvious they had significantly different approaches and had chosen different objectives for their statements. The team whose memo described the situation in negative terms of impending danger focused their rather explanatory communication on trust and confidence-building, emphasising the need for more information and staying clear of suggestions for concrete actions. Having felt trust and faith placed in their abilities from the wording of the CEO's brief, which focused on opportunity, the other group felt less pressure and produced a statement that contained clear actions and ideas radiating confidence, generally broadcasting their will to turn the situation around.

This little experiment gives a glimpse into the influence and potential that is hidden in the positive framing of internal communications. It creates a head-start in eliminating the negative connotations we associate with the term crisis and produces trust-based encouragement in your employees to work through a difficult time together. Relabelling crisis in your internal communications gives you an advantage in your response to a critical situation and can produce a high level of engagement and creativity, fostering a reinvention mindset. The same is true for external communications, and here I want to place particular emphasis on the tactic of inducing fear. While this is arguably the most relevant in crisis risk communication, I have found it equally important to consider in general communication in a crisis. Regardless of the actual risk involved, many managers deliberately apply frames of fear in their initial narrative to convey the severity of the situation and unite the audience in complying with measures. This can be commonly observed in politics and specifically during election campaigning.

Nevertheless, there is a fine line between doing this deliberately and missing the opportunity to change the frame, thus reinforcing the fear. When following one of the key principles of communicating effectively in a crisis – honesty – it might seem impossible to not reinforce fear. However, this doesn't have to be the case and can be dependent on the frame we apply. The more we stick to simple facts and focus on positive aspects when it comes to relational elements, the less we create assumptions that cause fear in the audience's mind. When communicating a risk, focus on the positive effects of following the recommendations or rules instead of the negative aspects of the risk itself. For example, when we communicate restrictions, it's important to focus upon what the positive outcome will be. This is different to why you are imposing them. If the personal impact on our audience is clear and relatable, it will significantly affect their motivation, endurance, and resilience. This is especially important, as crises have no specific end and can last for extended periods of time.

A PATH TO EFFECTIVE MESSAGING –
THE COMMUNICATION TRIANGLE

The concept of Stimmigkeit in communication can be translated as coherence, and it outlines the importance of having self-insight into how we're in a specific situation both emotionally and physically, something that is often referred to as authenticity. Additionally, Stimmigkeit focuses on the contextual layer required in terms of communication. Over the years, I found this concept highly effective in practice, and when analysing my own communication, I realised that I also work with a third element in focus: the audience. Context, audience, and I are the three core components I refer to as the Communication Triangle. This model helps me look at what and how I want to communicate from different angles, thus enabling me to design messages that take into consideration these three lenses. In doing so, I create space for manoeuvring where I place emphasis at what point, which makes my communication flexible and adaptable to either of the elements of the triangle.

Figure 2 – Communication Triangle

SELF: TAKING AN HONEST LOOK IN THE MIRROR

Whether as crisis managers, team members, decision-makers, or individuals in everyday life, communication always starts with us. Having the ability to assess ourselves is the foundation of deciding how and what we communicate. Self-reflection must go beyond any role or function and focus on the person behind it. This requires us to be in touch with our emotions and our responses to the context. It also requires reflecting on previous experiences and whether they influence or affect us because different crises can trigger different things in us, including unwanted memories. Through the years, I've noticed that everything seems to slow down for me during high-stress situations. I become calmer and I'm at ease. However, if I'm honest with myself, I can't generalise my reactions as applicable to all situations when I'm faced with a crisis. None of us can, and contrary to frequently proposed ideas, how we were affected by a previous crisis isn't a trustworthy indicator of how the next one will impact us. So, I take a pause to reflect: *How am I in this very moment?*

This is a seemingly simple question but one which I regularly ask myself when communicating, especially during crises. When sitting back in that longhouse in Borneo, the honest answer was lost. Observing the people around me and knowing what I was about to tell them made me want to vanish into thin air. I had no idea how to convey a message that wasn't going to be positive regardless of the angle adopted. I had no idea what to do next. Answering this question honestly can reveal some truths that might seem inconvenient in the moment (and even harder to face when we're in the role of crisis manager), but the realisations will benefit us in the aftermath and the long run, which is precisely what makes them of utmost importance for us and everyone around us. Having to deliver the news to the people who had welcomed and hosted me so kindly, I knew that I was afraid, and explicitly acknowledging this feeling relieved me of the internal pressure that arose from suppressing it.

Once we accept our own vulnerability, our fallibility, and the limitations inherent to our scope of influence, we can turn these insights into strengths. They show us, for example, where we need support. They also give us an understanding of what type of information we lack and the things we need to monitor regarding our own wellbeing and behaviour. Self-clarification is a fundamental pillar of having confidence in your own state and the ability to speak and communicate from a strong personal foundation. It helps us formulate our messages because it provides us with one of the ingredients for the aforementioned coherence: being true to ourselves. As part of this process, I also want to underline something that isn't often said – or at least not explicitly enough. Walking away from managing a crisis is not and will never be a sign of weakness.

Reflection and getting to know ourselves is a process that is never finished; it demands regular practice. I encourage everyone not to wait until the next crisis to do this because when it does, there might not be the time to practice. I also encourage you to gain perspectives and perceptions on how you communicated in a situation to see whether your own feelings and self-assessment match that of your audience. This way you will increase your ability to self-reflect and thereby learn.

CONTEXT: MAKING SENSE OF THE SITUATION

Situations matter. They have a significant impact on our perceptions, actions, and interactions. I distinguish between normal contexts and open contexts. Normal contexts, such as funerals or greeting rituals, present a set frame for expectations and interactions. Open contexts are less clearly defined and categorised and require more flexibility in assessing them. Crises are extreme forms of the open context, leaving us with the need to find ways to quickly understand the situation to be able to communicate accordingly. Ignoring the significance and the impact they have on our interactions leads inevitably to shortcomings when we develop communication strategies.

The pure essence of a crisis is that things change. Thus, understanding the context to such an extent as it would be possible in calmer times is short-lived. The fact that the situation changes quickly is already an important fact to consider in a communication strategy. Context is also something that differs in scope, and a full-scale understanding of the overall context is hardly ever required or possible for effective communications. This insight allows us to focus on the core of the context and avoid diving too deep. Sometimes, it might be sufficient to only assess your situation, but think bigger. My rule of thumb is the onion principle: as with peeling onions, I try to look at the bigger system first and work layer by layer down to the context that is relevant for my decisions. These might not always be complementary (as in my initial example). I took a starting point in the overall situation for the Indigenous people in Borneo and had to deliver a clear message. However, this message had to be delivered to representatives during a personal invitation into their homes. The content of the message concerned the bigger context, but it was being delivered in a personal and seemingly disconnected setting. This made it difficult to find an appropriate moment in the wonderful experience they had created for me during my visit. Naturally, my message wasn't perfect, but it was delivered.

I also regularly remind myself that the perception we have of any given situational context will generally differ, as does the way we are affected by it in return. This interplay is dynamic and highly subjective. Ignoring this fact regularly leads to misunderstandings and communication gaps. To overcome this, I try to construct a common context. This allows me to communicate more evenly and increases the likelihood of delivering my message effectively. I apply this technique frequently and ask for perspectives and descriptions of how other people interpret situations, how they feel in connection to certain things, as well as share my own views and emotions. This way, realities expand naturally, allowing for more connected communication via overlap.

AUDIENCE: UNDERSTANDING THE MULTITUDE OF STAKEHOLDERS

The Norwegian health director provoked some comments when he showed up to a nationally televised briefing wearing a Hawaiian shirt to announce the implementation of serious restrictions due to the COVID-19 pandemic. He might have been true to himself in that situation, but he didn't consider the context and what effect such a presentation could potentially have on the perception of the seriousness of the situation. Furthermore, he didn't consider how the audience would react, and when his name is mentioned you still hear comments here and there about this Hawaiian shirt. This type of distraction must be avoided in a severe crisis. While it presents a rather entertaining example, the potentially negative consequences on perception, reputation, and loss of messaging due to distraction are extremely high.

Trying to understand your audience is potentially the most difficult aspect of the triangle and knowing our audience in a crisis is, arguably, even harder. In these situations, we regularly deal with a variety of stakeholders, each with a different stake in the crisis, aiming for different outcomes. Considering that messages are determined by the receiver this presents a real challenge when designing communication in a crisis. It is near impossible to satisfy everyone with one message during a crisis.

When managing a crisis, it is very common to get completely absorbed in the tasks at hand. It's almost like entering a parallel world, with its own reality, where it's easy to get lost and disconnect from the situation around us. Therefore, it's essential to regularly remind ourselves that our "crisis universe" is different from everyone else's. Moreover, people not involved in managing our crisis have their own perceptions and limited access to the information we do. This should be the starting point for any type of communication with any stakeholder during such situations. Trying to put ourselves into relevant stakeholders' shoes is a key step in designing our message, anticipating needs, and identifying potential insecurities. All the while, one should keep in mind that not everybody is equally informed and that identifying what they need to know helps design communication better tailored to and less focused on one's own reality. Here are the elements to overcome this challenge:

Identify connectors and dividers

Understanding who I am communicating with proved to be crucial in every single crisis that I have managed. Whether it was the local government official, the people most affected, or the media, I had to learn how to manage the different relationships. But how to reach a versatile audience with just one message? This required a sound understanding of my audience. While different stakeholders may have different needs, they also have commonalities, which are crucial to identify. Commonalities are my starting point, and I then tailor my messaging around them because it allows me to reach a broader audience. The messages are subsequently phrased around these common needs and interests to maintain the connection.

However, a common trap is to focus only on the commonalities. To truly understand how your audience works, you also need to consider what divides it. In a crisis, you are dealing with a multitude of stakeholders, and not all communication is, nor must be aimed at everyone. Looking at them as one can make us blind to individual needs, and we might overlook potential traps that can influence our messaging. Therefore, it's crucial to acknowledge and understand their differences. Ignoring what differentiates them can lead to unintended communication around a divider, thus only reaching a part of the population.

Furthermore, knowing what concerns them individually enables us to tailor our communication specifically to their needs when addressing this sub-audience directly. Identifying these differences can help us understand what to possibly exclude and what to emphasise in individual communication. Messages should be tailored to an audience's individuality yet target common needs at their core. For example, the stakeholders of a company that faces a crisis might include investors, board members, employees, and customers. While they certainly share commonalities, they come from very different positions and have diverse interests. Looking upon them as a homogenous group will limit communication and might implicitly address things that increase concerns rather than unite. To tailor our communication, analyse both connectors and dividers to increase options, make communication flexible, and reach the audience where they are.

Remember that you are part of the audience

Something that proves effective for me when preparing to communicate is to remind myself that I'm just as much part of the audience as I am the messenger. As crisis managers absorbed in our roles, we often overlook the simple truth that we're just as affected by the situation. Being able to empathically switch roles and look upon the situation from the audience's perspective can make a difference in terms of how effectively we communicate in a crisis.

It's helpful to think about how we would want to be informed about the situation ourselves. What is it we would like to hear? The answer gives an indicator of what the needs could be, how you could phrase your messaging, and what your level of focus relationally and/or factually should be.

The human factor is a key element of communication in a crisis. This requires an appropriate balance between an honest and fact-based communication style, as well as space for emotions and their acknowledgement, though honesty mustn't be mistaken for full disclosure. Through timely analysis and empathetic understanding of the context, traps like this one can be avoided. Ultimately, it's about maintaining trust and credibility, and while context and self-awareness build a strong foundation, mastering the communication triangle alongside framing considerations is a key differentiator in your communication.

SIX CONSIDERATIONS WHEN FRAMING COMMUNICATION IN CRISIS

Critical situations require new ways of thinking. Yet, whether it is writing the perfect CV for a friend, relationship advice, or a career change we are noticeably better at thinking innovatively and daring new approaches if it does not concern our own problems. Similarly, in a crisis, our focus quickly becomes very narrow. At one point or another, it might seem like we hit a wall and are looping around ourselves. Remember that letting go of the unrealistic ambition of formulating the perfect message is not only liberating but allows you to focus on elements that are within your control. Here are six considerations that can help you frame your message in a crisis:

1. Remember the message is always made on the receiver's end

Interpersonal and intergroup communications evolve around a sender-to-receiver principle with alternating roles. I studied communication psychology and applied many different approaches before I accepted this simple yet effective truth: no matter the intention with which you try to convey your message, it's only worth as much as the receiver gives you credit. Accepting this relieved me of the pressure of constantly trying to communicate perfectly. It's important to acknowledge that there are limitations to our communication – one of them being the ability to design a perfect message – because there will always be someone who reads different things into what you're trying to communicate, or someone who interprets your actions completely backwards. The likelihood of this happening in crises is even higher due to their emotional nature.

When communicating in crises, it is also highly relevant to consider other psychological phenomena, namely the confirmation bias and the selective perception bias. The former leads us to naturally develop an understanding of reality and subconsciously look for arguments and facts that support this image. The latter differs to the fact that we see what we expect to see. Therefore, once our reality has been shaped, we are selective in our interpretation of all messages – or their elements – in a way that feeds into our perception of the crisis and seems helpful in our respective emotional states. Combined, these two biases present a potential spiral that is created and reinforced through implicit messages. I learned to practice being explicit in my messaging because it reduces the likelihood of assumptions and leaves as little as possible subject to interpretation to avoid misunderstandings.

A good example is again the use of recommendations instead of rules during a crisis. The underlying intention isn't to send the message of overregulation but to signal trust in people being able to choose the "right" option. Only that part is left implied. Looking at the term recommendation alone, the decision lies with the person or people to which it's given. This is highly dependent on what the person makes of it. If someone is very loyal to authority and has a strong sense of the collective, they might be more inclined to interpret a recommendation as being closer to a rule than to a choice. People with a strong sense of freedom, a different political affiliation, and/ or an individualistic mindset might hear it as their own free decision. This frequently causes misunderstandings, frustrations, a split in the population, and makes crisis communication highly ineffective. I have stopped working with recommendations and clearly allocate the responsibility where it is. I explain when a situation is not a rule but a strong recommendation due to, say, a legal limitation, where the responsibility lies, and what I expect of the audience.

2. Balance emotions and facts

The importance of balance, as a model related to many ancient and Indigenous philosophies, plays a central role in my crisis management work and approach. This means that elements, values, and actions should be balanced in such a way as not to negatively exaggerate their significance. This is important when it comes to communication where a balance is needed between stating facts and acknowledging emotions. Often, facts are hard to come by in a crisis, particularly in the early stages, yet they have a calming and reassuring effect because they eliminate uncertainty and assumptions about the unknown. Even if the facts aren't what people hoped for, they are better than speculations about what's happening or how the situation will develop.

On the other hand, emotions are important to acknowledge because they often present a key barrier to communicating important messages, including emotional blockers (whether positive or negative) that need to be overcome. For example, there is a fine line between acknowledgement and overcommunication of empathy – which can turn into a perception of inauthenticity – and mastering this is incredibly difficult because it differs from crisis to crisis and requires the ability to sense your audience. What makes this even more challenging is that emotions change during the lifecycle of a crisis. When communicating in a crisis, it's important to develop a feeling for timing and mood. Sometimes it's helpful to start with ourselves and assess our own emotional state. It's crucial to read our audience and assess whether you need to make space for emotions, or if the receivers are ready for facts. This will often require a balance because people have extremely different responses and needs in crisis situations.

3. Have a sales pitch mindset

Time and again, too many details are shared when communicating in a crisis. The reasons for this are manyfold but commonly relate to a mental model stipulating that information creates trust and explains decisions. Rarely is either the case. It's impossible for any stakeholder to follow overly detailed information. This, in turn, contributes to undermining trust and increasing vulnerability because we might get confused by our own level of detail and can be criticised when mixing up information. More importantly, however, it distracts from the core message.

I learned this the hard way when I started my own business and had to develop communication and messages regarding the company's vision, services, and how it supports potential clients. I underestimated how difficult it is to boil it down to its essence when you know too much about something. What I learned in that experience is easily transferable to a crisis context. Approach your communication like a sales pitch: everyone should be able to understand it and repeat it simply, so focus on the key elements and remember you have limited time to convey your key messages. Taking this into consideration, the focus will always be on what it is that the audience needs to know first.

If I have the luxury, I test my approach first with an audience that I trust and that isn't involved in the development of the messaging and communication strategy. This is even more important when the audience is required to act based on what is explained. During the pandemic, many countries introduced systems, such as traffic lights to indicate infection rates and restrictions. However, in almost all countries, people didn't immediately understand the system, which led to confusion and required further clarification. If you use such an approach, it's beneficial to test it out because while it might seem logical to you, the world looks quite different outside a crisis management team than it does inside it. Finally, it's important to remember that we have a short attention span – even more so in critical situations. I design my messages so that the most important thing is communicated first. This way, I not only ensure there is no doubt about what I want to emphasise, but it also creates a reference point that I can return to repeatedly.

4. Avoid the justification trap

You might know the feeling of trying to explain something but failing to get your message across and perhaps even facing resistance. When we reflect on how we handle this, we might realise that we're prone to using different ways to explain what we mean. This, paradoxically, often diffuses the message further and gives the receiver more options to interpret or misinterpret what you wanted to communicate, thus making us vulnerable in our messaging. In crises, clarity and simple comprehension are some of the pillars of effective communication.

In my early days managing crises, I noticed a tendency to use too many words and details to make sure that stakeholders understood the reasoning behind my decisions. While I was trying to compensate with information overload not to make myself vulnerable, the exact opposite became the case. I received a lot of questions about irrelevant details rather than the actual decisions. Similar things can often be observed in press conferences or statements made by companies in crisis situations.

Step by step, I started to understand that this isn't necessary, that less is more, and that you can always provide further details later. Our audience primarily wants to know what was decided and how we got to this decision. However, it's an incredibly fine line between an explanation and a justification. Mastering it is an art that requires practice and feedback on performance. If in doubt, I apply the "need to know/nice to know" test. In other words, does it make a difference if the audience knows this information? If your answer is no, you can leave this out of your communication; if the answer is a yes or maybe, ask yourself the following question: "What would be the added value for them by knowing this?" It's crucial that you answer this for the audience and not yourself. This simple test can already reduce parts of your messaging that adds to confusion rather than clarity and trust.

5. Prioritise internal communication

When a crisis evolves, there is generally a focus on external communications especially in connection to reputation management and public relations. In my experience, this creates a blind spot.

Everything starts on the inside, and this should be prioritised. Reputation is closely connected to how the crisis is dealt with internally, something that's often underestimated. Whether it's a large company, an organisation, or a small business, internal communications hold the key to successfully managing a crisis through the *power of inclusion* and the *creation of transparency*.

The power of ensuring inclusion

Have you ever been in a situation where you were presented with a decision and you thought, Do I not get a say in this? It concerns me as well. When you're the one to regularly inform employees about crucial developments, steps, and decisions, ensure they are not presented as final but rather as a possible option, even if you might have already made a specific choice. If the possible choices are presented openly with the invitation for input, this can have a positive effect on engagement and ownership. One of the biggest challenges in a crisis is feeling like we lost or are about to lose control. Presenting definite and unchangeable information and decisions will contribute to intensifying that feeling. However, presenting ideas and the approach that was chosen as the way forward and welcoming opinions and thoughts that you ensure will be considered will increase commitment, participation, and ownership of the process and decisions.

It is crucial to keep your internal structures and systems stable, as they are already threatened from the outside through the crisis your organisation is facing. Creating more insecurity and uncertainty internally through a lack of sufficient communication can cause an additional crisis and further destabilisation. People have a natural tendency to want to help if they feel they can contribute, are given space to do so, and are regularly informed about progress. If they are involved by an invitation to participate through ideas, you keep control over your whole team internally and over concise communications externally.

The significance of creating transparency

In critical situations, specific teams are formed to deal with challenges. This means regular long hours and high-paced processes in combination with high-stakes. Additionally, they are expected to manage huge amounts of information in an adrenalin-induced atmosphere, which is somewhat of a separate reality. Whilst being caught up in the crisis and having to deal with myriad dilemmas and decisions, other things are left to the wayside including internal communications. This is where a dangerous homemade trap is created: the longer a crisis continues without information being shared internally, the more detrimental the impact can be on the company.

Humans are naturally drawn to and interested in things that are scarce, mysterious, and secretive. Everything that is exclusive has more attraction than what is freely and readily available. I have witnessed a similar effect in crisis management. Everything that happens on a crisis management team seems mysterious and exciting to everyone else. Being a part of the team on the inside, however, it is easy to forget that the world on the outside continues to exist. Employees observe, discuss, and naturally fill the void of information with bits and pieces they think they have heard from somewhere, and before we know it, there is the potential for a completely different version of the situation than what we are busy managing to become subject of internal speculations.

In critical times, we need the trust and support of the people that surround us (along with other stakeholders), and transparency is an effective way of building just that. However, transparency isn't the same as full disclosure. In some crises, information is sensitive, however, no matter the crisis, there is always something that can be shared, even if it's as simple as an update that the crisis team has met and when the rest of the organisation and colleagues can expect more information. This creates a feeling of being considered and included, even if not as an active member of the crisis team because many of us need to be assured that we're not forgotten in a crisis. Regularly sharing information can contribute to this feeling of solidarity and gain you trust, support, and loyalty while navigating uncertainty and reducing doubt. It's essential to avoid the scenario where crisis management and subsequently crisis communication becomes an exclusive club with little to no external access.

Our team is the single biggest pool of resources we have at the start, during, and in the aftermath of a crisis. We become too strongly focused on external actors and stakeholders and forget the ones that sit within the company – those that are closest to us. It's our responsibility not only to keep them informed but to also discover and stimulate their potential in these situations. I live by the principle that my team should never be informed about any important decisions via anyone else but myself. Avoiding a situation wherein employees or team members learn crucial information affecting them and the company from others can prevent serious obstacles when managing a crisis. These typically include the likelihood of having to deal with interpretations, reactions, and disappointments that they weren't entrusted with the information directly. Dealing with any of these ultimately costs more energy and time than it would have to simply inform your staff directly. This isn't only a misplacement of focus and flawed prioritisation, but its implied message can have a severe impact on the relationship as well as the loyalty and commitment.

6. Adjust your strategy over time

Communication in crisis must be adjusted regularly and over time, as the context and the situation evolve constantly. The dynamic nature of a crisis and its often fast-changing context quickly requires adjustment to the decisions that need to be made and the way we communicate about them. This doesn't allow for too much dwelling on things that were previously said, leading to a natural form of deflection. When using deflection in your communication, you distract from the actual topic by directing the communication to a different one. In crises, this is naturally facilitated due to a dynamic context giving crisis managers the chance to redeem and learn. Yet, I have noticed the latter is where crisis managers often struggle. In crises learning and adjustment are down-prioritised by comparison to activities in response to changes in the context.

After two years of COVID-19 being a global pandemic, governments have, in many ways, still failed to adjust the communication strategies used when the crisis hit initially. This also means that things that were unsuccessful in the crisis communication early on are still being repeated, resulting in a loss of trust because the audience is less forgiving to mistakes made when the ones making them don't show the ability to learn from them. The Norwegian government, for example, used the same messaging one year after the first restrictions were declared, emphasising the spirit of collectively working to fight this crisis. A year into it, this narrative had lost relevance and credibility, leading to the opposite response of what was intended.

As crises have no clear end, they require continued communication beyond the crisis to include and address other effects and potential consequential crises, ensuring that stakeholders' needs and interests are being considered. Communication in crisis is complicated and mustn't be underestimated. It is often organic and can develop in accordance with the situation itself. It is essential to acknowledge that it can hardly ever be done perfectly due to the complexity and the dynamism of the environment around it. Consideration, self-awareness and an understanding of one's audience and context can help you frame your messages flexibly and in line with the changing situation.

Throughout my life and career, I've had numerous encounters like the one in Malaysia. Sometimes, it was the context or me that stood in the way of effective communication. Other times, I made the wrong assumptions about the audience, and most of the time, I didn't consider the triangle and its dynamic. We must accept that we never fully own how communication plays out and its effects. Many elements are beyond our control, and all we can do is simply focus on trying to consider them to the extent possible when we tailor our messages. They will never be perfect, and arguably that is what makes communication such an exciting and frustrating topic. However, we have plenty of room within this triangle to choose and play with our messages. When communicating, I usually adopt the audience's perspective and follow a piece of Indigenous advice: Observe, listen, learn.

KEY TAKE-AWAYS

▶ Communication moves in feedback loops, and it's important that you assess how you are before and during communicating.

▶ Simply hearing the term crisis can trigger something in us, and we can show unexpected emotional responses.

▶ Contexts are being perceived differently, and to reduce the chance of misunderstandings and disconnected communication, try to design a common context with your audience by exchanging your perceptions.

▶ When studying your audience, look at what connects and divides them. This way, you can avoid further dividing them through your messages, and you'll be able to tailor specific messages to specific groups. It's also helpful to remember that you are part of the audience.

▶ Honesty when communicating doesn't mean fully disclosing everything. It merely means that what is said must be truthful to avoid potential backlash.

▶ Think of your messaging like a sales pitch, short and with the most important message in the beginning. As such, everyone should be able to repeat the message at the end of the communication.

▶ When you're in doubt about what to add to your message, apply the "nice to know/need to know test." This helps you filter out the information that might not be essential at this point in time. Remember to take the audience's perspective.

PART II
CRAFT

#1 BUILD A FOUNDATION
FOR REINVENTION

W hen I walked into the house – technically no more than a shed of corrugated iron plates – I thought I was prepared for what I was about to see. I had heard stories about the South African townships and their living conditions and realised as soon as I walked through the makeshift door that the images I had built from stories were as far from the truth as possible. I had never seen poverty of that sort before in my life and hadn't been able to picture it, let alone people living in it. The images are burned into my memory, and I will never forget them. I saw basic assets – a mattress, a gas cooker, and a broken shelf with a radio on top of it. The owner of the house, an elderly lady, was sitting in what seemed to be her most precious possession – her rocking chair. Through my colleague, who was also her nephew, she told me with great pride about the neighbourhood and her house. I was still trying to take in the images when she asked me if I wanted to see the other room. I looked around, not sure I understood because I couldn't see another door. Then she pointed to a hole in the corner, which I had mistaken for a natural toilet, and told me to have a look. I looked down into what I would have described as an improvised cave where I also saw a mattress, a gas cooker, and some clothes. My host told me this was where her tenant lived, a young man who happened to come home not long after she had told me about him. He sat with us and shared that he couldn't afford to live anywhere else, as he wouldn't be able to afford his studies if the rent were any higher. He said he was appreciative for this home because it allowed him to get an education and that he would be eternally grateful to the old lady, whom he referred to in the traditional way as "auntie." This encounter worked for years within me, and I often wonder what became of this young man. I was too inexperienced back then to comprehend what I had witnessed, but over the years, witnessing many similar situations, some more extreme and others less so, I started to understand that resilience is the foundation that paves our way through a crisis by means of reinvention.

DESIGN YOUR OWN JOURNEY

Crises present a vacuum, and many crises have brought about incredible insights and innovations that might have taken a lot longer to discover had the desperation not opened the door to new ways of thinking and trying out things. Crises make us feel overwhelmed because of the dynamic context, the ever-changing situation, and the insecurity related to how to best deal with them. More specifically, they are moments when change is inevitable and will happen regardless of what we decide. The difference stands in the level of impact. Crises are peaks of constant development that we experience when changes happen at a larger scale elevated in speed and impact. They tend to result from a combination of external factors and internal processes where crucial decisions have been avoided for too long.

Every crisis also comes with options that are predetermined by the situation. So, if we have options, where do the frustration we often experience and the perceived feeling of helplessness that takes over come from? It's precisely the fact that we're not the ones who chose these options that leads to feeling a step behind. Predetermined options can distract us from coming to the realisation that this is a perfect moment to create our own solutions, where our instincts lead us to look for ways to solve the situation. In other words, there is no better moment to reinvent ourselves or our organisations than in a crisis, where regardless of the outcome, something will change significantly. However, the opportunity to create new options is frequently dismissed because it's perceived as adding risk to an already difficult situation. Yet, this perception feeds into helplessness, thus completing the proverbial catch-22.

It's important to remember that risk perception is highly subjective. Risks are connected to every single choice we make in critical times, and the bigger the feeling of risk, the likelier it is to lead to greater change. Therefore, it is understandable that investing in innovation during a crisis can often be dismissed by being perceived as too risky by adding more unknowns to the unknown. Many times, I heard something along these lines: "At least, with this choice, we know where we're heading." However, knowing where we're heading, or the perception that's the case, doesn't necessarily mean this will always be the actual destination – that we will get there in one piece, the same way, or all together. In reality, it's almost never possible to predict the outcome of a decision because we assume the effect of our decision-making though we can't know for sure how it will impact our situation. Therefore, we must be clear on how we make our choices and why we make them.

Focusing on risks in a crisis is focusing mainly on survival, and this is a rather passive way of dealing with the situation. Survival, however, can be covered by ensuring business continuity while the crisis is dealt with and used for reinvention, where you look upon how you do things from different perspectives within your business with the aim of creating new and innovative approaches. How a crisis is responded to makes the difference between the situation being a missed opportunity or a golden chance. Reinvention allows companies to create their own options and develop innovative solutions for their specific problems based on available resources to not only survive a critical moment but use it to reinvent themselves and move forward.

BUILD RESILIENCE AS A FOUNDATION FOR REINVENTION

Reinvention is a proactive approach to managing a crisis, with the aim of using it as a fresh start, an opportunity, and the chance to decide to shape our future selves. The foundation that enables this approach is resilience, and I believe that each of us is born with natural resilience. I've seen and experienced resilience in many forms, having worked with Indigenous communities, with forcibly displaced populations and other peoples that have lived in the context of conflict for their entire lives. I have also experienced the importance of resilience in crises I faced personally; therefore, I refrain from a general definition of the concept, as it's highly individual and cultural. It does, however, come with the ability to learn from adversity.

"Resilience has many faces."
– Anisa Goshi

For organisations, the magic ingredient to resilience is culture. Organisational culture is a broad term, which includes processes, plans, systems, approaches, communications, and mindsets, as well as knowledge and learning. I have supported leaders and organisations over the years in building resilience and resilient cultures. As a result, I have noticed six elements that stand out as core pillars for successfully increasing resilience and opening the way for active reinvention during a crisis:

Habit 1: Make your purpose your anchor
When we try to proactively shape our future during a crisis, we are also quick to question our purpose and motivation for why we do what we do. While this can be useful at times, it's also one of the biggest contributors to an increased sense of uncertainty. The first

piece of advice I almost always give in critical situations is based on what I call the Linus principle: find an anchor. This principle is inspired by Peanuts, a famous comic strip that ran from the 1950s to the year 2000. Charlie Brown's best friend is a boy named Linus, who is most famous for a blanket that he takes with him anywhere and everywhere. This is a beautiful portrayal of what we often see particularly in young children if they are in moments of transition; they usually carry something with them. It's literally something to hold on to that serves as an anchor whose only function is to provide a sense of security, stability, and control.

An anchor can be anything from a ritual, a song, a phrase, to any type of object. The sole purpose of it is to provide grounding and refocus on the here and now as the only space and time where we can influence things. Our purpose is one of the most effective anchors in a crisis. Ironically, the drive behind why we do what we do frequently takes the back seat to all our activities, and whilst it's somehow always there, the more we follow a routine, the less explicit it becomes. Sometimes, the loss of a sense of purpose is one of the core reasons contributing to the birth of a crisis. Our purpose can and should serve as the anchor to fall back on, get motivation and security from, and act as a reminder of why it's important to find a way through the situation. It's important to clarify and regularly make our purpose explicit to help find stability and grounding when we're faced with a crisis.

Habit 2: Apply creative flexibility

One way or another, we all live and structure our lives following routines. Personally, I don't like routines, but I see their necessity in certain situations. Crises, as I lay out in the chapter on readiness, are not automatically amongst them. Routines build on plans and standard operating procedures. Yet, as the name indicates, they present a standard, and this standard can block innovation. So, where to find the middle ground? The answer is habits. Habits have the advantage of satisfying our need for routine because the core of the habit is the same. However, their execution can differ significantly. To achieve this, we must carry them out creatively, and I always work with this creative flexibility as a core principle to help avoid severe disruption during crises. Flexibility means not needing a predefined approach for how a situation should be handled. Whether it's a plan or a protocol, they must be looked upon primarily as guidance that can be consulted when in doubt or when feeling stuck but not as a standard in any crisis. I work with the attitude of understanding the context and identifying the problem first, then deciding how to solve it. This way, I ensure flexibility and an unbiased crisis management approach, which caters to reinvention.

Habit 3: Ensure continuous competency development
Our competencies increase constantly throughout our lifetime. Much of it happens without us noticing, yet we also deliberately engage in activities to boost them. I consider it essential to develop our competencies regularly, to increase our personal skillset and be better equipped for turbulent times. By this, I don't necessarily mean competencies that are relevant for crisis management because, as I point out in the chapter on resources, everything is a potential resource in a crisis, which means that your language course in Chinese might come in handy in a situation without knowing this will be the case beforehand, so I encourage any kind of skill development. Organisations that want to become more resilient and facilitate reinvention opportunities must consider all employees eligible for training. This way, they create skillsets that are cross-cutting and allow for different forms of cooperation. Furthermore, they become less vulnerable because the competency doesn't lie with specific people. Additionally, it reduces the impact of losing certain

competencies due to staff turnover. The healthy side effect of this open approach is that staff members are given appreciation through the provision of the opportunity for competency development, potentially strengthening loyalty and cohesion.

It is important to make competency development a continuous activity. Like muscles that take time to respond when not flexed regularly, competencies need to be worked on habitually. One-time interventions – and I have led way too many of them – are insufficient to be considered effective competency development. It is unprofessional and bordering on insulting if we assume that we all become masters in active listening through a one-day course. As with all competencies, they require practice and repetition, so it's imperative to have ongoing competency development that is supplemented by a combination of more training and practical applications.

Habit 4: Identify ways to learn effectively

A frequently underestimated part of a resilient culture is the ability to learn. This includes not only gathering insights after certain events but also refers to an organisation's ability to constantly learn by applying these insights into what does and doesn't work, creating ways to utilise this knowledge and employing these measures in real-time. Effective learning translates into behaviour. As with competency development, we tend to learn through one-time tick-box exercises after events have taken place, but learning is highly subjective and a continuous process. Learning must be an integrative part of crisis management to turn insights into competencies and make implicit processes explicit. Through an open, regular, and clear approach to learning, we will become better equipped to deal with fast-changing environments and more adaptive to the dynamics surrounding them. It will also enable us to find different paths to solve problems and pave the way to reinvention. It's less about learning from the past for the future and more about making learning a constant part of our work, not allowing it to become a disruptive and disconnected exercise. I want to stress that the most important learning from a crisis is in what worked well because that's what got us through it. This allows us to identify things that we do well which in turn can be resources for future situations. Therefore, focusing on the successful elements of crisis management must constitute the first step of learning from a crisis.

Habit 5: Foster a reinventor's mentality

Being ready for a crisis and having the necessary resilience and endurance to deal with challenging periods is rooted more in a mindset than in any other skill. A crisis hardly ever follows a predictable curve of its life cycle and in many ways, it doesn't have a beginning or a clear ending. This requires a mentality that demystifies and transforms the term crisis into an incentive to work towards permanently being ready to throw everything on the table and reshaping something new out of it. This is deeply entrenched in the way we communicate in relation to innovation and reinvention, whether as an individual or part of an organisation. The way we talk about a situation reveals our attitude from the outset. Fostering an attitude that strives for reinvention and exploring how to do things differently requires regular encouragement and positive framing. A reinventor's mindset isn't only relevant in a crisis but a key catalyst for steady personal and professional development.

Habit 6: Always look for alternative solutions

How we communicate shapes our mindset, yet it's just one piece of the puzzle. If we're not actively trying to develop and realise new ideas, reinvention will remain wishful thinking and noble ambition during a crisis. We might not be used to working innovatively, and in times of uncertainty, we fall back on the things we know. That said, if we practice innovation and different approaches regularly, this becomes the natural way of working and what we'll fall back on when facing a crisis. To practice this, we must deliberately make space for developing the habit of thinking about and finding alternative solutions. When I design crisis management strategies, workshops, or other processes, I regularly drive the people I work with insane by asking the question "How could we do this completely differently?" After a while, the same thing happens every single time. At one point, I'm the one faced with exactly this question, which means that the habit has started to settle in and manifest.

I believe we are all born with innate resilience. Watching children interact with constant uncertainty as they learn, shows that it's essential not to forget that we have these skills. In crises, we naturally adapt to the situation. What makes the difference is finding ways to use this difficult experience to write our own narrative instead of it being written for us. It's all about learning to turn the challenge into an advantage. If we foster resilience both inside and around, we'll be equipped to take what feels like a risk and embark on a journey to reinvention.

KEY TAKE-AWAYS

▶ What's on the other side of a crisis, if we approach it in a reactive manner, will be decided for us. An active way to approach a crisis is via the path of reinvention.

▶ One of the most effective ways to get ready for a crisis is through cultural resilience.

▶ Instead of questioning and overthrowing your purpose, use it as an anchor, a starting point, and a driver of motivation to get you through the uncertain times.

▶ The key to effectively learning from a crisis lies in looking at what worked well and how you managed to get through it. What you will find are the qualities that make you resilient, which present valuable resources for the future.

▶ Continuously improve your competencies because they all turn into resources during difficult times.

▶ Resilience, endurance, and reinventive ability are all deeply rooted in our mindset. All of these traits can be trained and built over time. The way we communicate about a crisis sets the tone for how we will manage it. It's important to approach it with an attitude that's positive at its core and focuses on the options rather than the obstacles.

#2 DEEP-DIVE
INTO RESOURCES

The room was full of gum boots, rubber gloves and skiing glasses. The randomness of these items struck me. The room, however, was set up with impeccable attention to detail. Every bucket had its place, every position was marked on the floor, and every helper knew what they had to do – and did just that. This was part of a training seminar that had become extremely popular amongst humanitarians in 2014 during the devastating outbreak of the Ebola virus in West Africa. It was developed by an organisation that had dealt with previous outbreaks, and what seemed like a weird collection of tools for a costume party was in fact experience-based life-saving equipment. Teams that worked with Ebola previously and understood its deadliness had to find ways to protect themselves and use the resources they had available and that were possible to disinfect and cleanse without being destroyed. This resulted in some of the things being used in a completely different way than originally intended and for a fundamentally different purpose. The Ebola response in many ways showed how important it is to understand, know, and reinvent your resources.

EVERYTHING IS A RESOURCE

One of the heroes of my youth was MacGyver, titular protagonist of the legendary TV show from the '80s and '90s. His superpower was to find solutions – most of them involving his pocketknife – in what seemed like hopeless situations. His readiness was unparalleled not out of preparedness but as a result of resourcefulness. As with many of my friends, I also had a pocketknife of that sort back then. I no longer carry it but have since had an interest in survival skills and creativity. Luckily, most people never experience situations where they have to fight for their very survival. Yet, the crises we face trigger similar responses in us and require a MacGyver mindset to respond to them. Simplified, this means that we must consider that everything is a potential resource in a crisis. This mindset consists of eliminating blind spots, discovering hidden resources, and finding alternative ways to use them. To adopt a MacGyver mindset, you need to train and practice a few core principles.

Principle 1: What I have is all I need

When we experience helplessness and feel like we are losing control, we tend to forget and ignore our resources. Each of us has a lot of experience, skills, knowledge, and ideas, all of which can be essential in critical situations. Yet, in crises, we are quick to aim for more resources and envy those who do seemingly have endless things at their disposal. This focus is misleading. It makes us believe we are ill-equipped and distracts us from the fact that we already have plenty that is available. In a crisis, everything is and must absolutely be looked upon as a resource, ranging from a person, their skillsets, experience, knowledge, and potential, to the more materialistic things such as money and assets, as well as time and connections. Everything can potentially help us, so it's crucial to know what we have at our disposal.

Furthermore, when talking about resources or assets, we tend to forget invisible skills and factors, such as mental health, motivation, commitment, and creativity. These elements are all closely linked to one's mindset. They can be differentiators and have a severe impact on how a crisis is being managed because a motivated team will be more determined and committed to exploring what is on the other side of uncertainty regardless of the outcome, just like embracing and believing in my creative side will most likely help me find alternative options to deal with the challenges ahead. Employees who feel like they belong are more likely to be loyal at critical times. These overlooked resources become even more powerful as they can be fostered and developed.

When working in humanitarian crises, I was always dependent on drivers. At the beginning of my career, I was told that drivers will be the most important people with whom I would work. This was one of many great pieces of advice I was lucky to get from experienced field veterans. However, it wasn't until the first critical situation at a checkpoint that I understood the truth, depth, and importance of that statement. It meant that a driver is never "just" a driver – that they are people with vast experience and a set of resources, whether languages, information, wisdom, connections, or loyalty that might not all be relevant for the core of their tasks but that can become relevant in any situation. And drivers are just one example; the same can be true of any other role in an organisation.

For this reason, though the results may never be comprehensive, I have created and now work with a resource grid that allows me to identify gaps and reduce the potential of overlooking valuable elements in crisis management. Such an overview also contributes to confidence and facilitates an increased sense of having options. The mapping is ideally a light and informal process to allow you to access your resources with an open mind and reduced bias. I like to work in subtle ways that not only allow for team members to share their experiences and expertise but also provide insight into what is available beyond what's visible daily. Considering ourselves and the people around us as magic baskets of resources can prove to be a game-changer. It naturally expands our zone of leverage and enables us to create new options in critical times.

When you develop your resource overview, separate them in categories and where possible be specific before plotting them onto the grid. The resource grid serves as an overview to ensure a clear picture of what you have at hand. You'll also be able to identify blind spots and create awareness about resources that are limited and need to be regularly maintained, recharged, or used with care. Repeat this exercise regularly as resources change.

Steps:

• List as many of your resources as you can think of.
• Plot them on the grid in the respective squares.
• Discuss blind spots, assumptions, and misallocations.

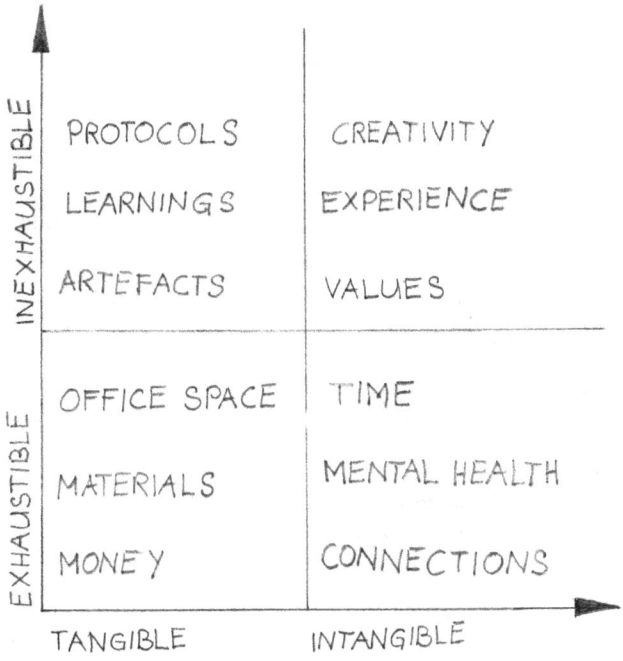

Figure 3 – Resource Grid

Principle 2: My resources change constantly

Resource inventories reveal that our resources change constantly. We acquire new ones while losing others. As outlined above, resources consist of different elements, many of which are related to our personal experiences and skillsets and all of which can become important in a potential crisis, which by their nature are also catalysts for this development. The intensity, dynamic, and weight of such situations are all elements that significantly elevate our experience. If we capture the experience and learn from it, we come out more resourceful on the other end of a crisis than when first faced with it. These reflections will contribute to our experience, knowledge, and other potentially enriching learnings that can be added to or removed from our resource inventory and overall capacity.

Repeating the aforementioned exercise is also helpful with a specific focus on a problem or challenge. Clarity on tasks can contribute to a more specific mapping. This might lead to new opportunities, thus significantly increasing options. This exercise needs to be inclusive and transparent; otherwise, it might just create or reiterate initial blind spots and still leave key resources undetected. However, there is also a potential downside to doing this with a specific problem in mind. It narrows the focus, and the likelihood of falling back on the resources that were used in similar situations is high. This directly affects the development of innovative and new solutions. Therefore, it's important to identify and test assumptions and mental models in this situation. No matter the circumstances, we must always assume we will be unable to get additional resources and that what we have is all we will have to work with. Everything else will be a bonus, though initially, we must practice a MacGyver mindset to be ready to handle the next critical situation creatively with the resources that are at our disposal.

Principle 3: Be considerate with resources

Identifying our resources and being able to reinvent them is one side of the story. The other is ensuring we're not running out of them during a crisis and that we're recharging, maintaining, and stocking up on some of them during and after handling a critical situation. Crisis management is about being considerate about how we use our resources. This applies to both tangible and non-tangible resources, while the latter are usually more difficult to identify, thus frequently overlooked. Sometimes, crises will last for a long period of time and demand a lot from the people involved in dealing with the situation. Therefore, it's important to find ways to reduce the waste of resources through misallocation or overuse. It's impossible to completely avoid the fact that some efforts turn out unsuccessful and resources occasionally fail to yield significant results; however, my experience has taught me that a resource map and the creation of options based on what is available reduces reservoir depletion.

Another factor here is the appropriateness of resources. We're quick to use a lot of resources to respond to a situation. However, it's important to remember that the resources we use to deal with a crisis will be taken from elsewhere. If we focus our attention on one thing, we have less capacity to deal with something else. Similarly, in organisations where top-level managers assume they need to be in crisis management teams. They of course can, though it comes at a price. Their normal responsibilities and business continuity does get undervalued, so such situations need to be thoroughly reflected, and decisions need to be made with consideration.

Principle 4: Find alternative ways to use your resource

One of the things I admire most about survival experts is their resourcefulness and ability to reinvent things. They manage to turn something that seems completely useless into the magic ingredient to solve a hopeless situation in the most challenging environments. It turns out this isn't so much a practical skill as it is a mindset and mental ability. The secret lies in being able to constantly imagine the alternate ways you could make use of something. We're all natural reinventors, but we forget (or wholly fail to recognize) how often we use this gift. Some might call it adjusting while others call it coping, but regardless of the term, each of us adapts to a crisis and learns to live with it. This is a natural survival instinct that helps us to find ways to deal with a critical situation. These things are often so small that we don't notice them immediately, yet we all possess them.

Reinvention is primarily the ability to break down and free oneself from mental models, the strong assumptions that help us make sense of our environment and how to interact with it. They include the understanding of various approaches, how to use objects, and how things do or don't work. For example, we attribute specific functions to certain objects. If we look at a spoon, most of us will immediately think of a tool that facilitates eating. However, there are many more functions for spoons ranging from musical instruments to weapons; the list is long. An open mindset stops us from allowing only one or a few mental models to dominate the assessment of what else we could do with any given subject or skill.

There is, however, a fine line between developing this skill and overusing it. Reinvention mustn't be mistaken for invention. What I notice people and businesses do time and again is misguidedly throw everything out and adopt a wildly different approach. What happens in these situations is that the focus has shifted from the actual resources at hand to the wider context including resources that aren't at our disposal at the time. I've seen organisations that didn't survive crises because of their ambition to come up with the one idea that saves the situation. It's crucial to look at what you have before trying to start over from scratch, which often results in fragmented and uncoordinated crisis management. I encourage you to practice this mind shift regularly whether alone or on a team. In my work, I train this through the habitual identification of assumptions and blind spots. This includes methods that push you to think differently and reinvent yourself and your way of working. Develop this skill not with the aim to constantly reinvent but to train your reinvention muscle, allowing you to quickly break down mental models and develop new options.

Crises trigger our survival instincts. Each of us is packed with resources because of our different skills, experiences, and how we perceive the world. Having contact and awareness of how vast they are and that they're constantly changing is such a powerful advantage in difficult times because it naturally presents us with more options. If we manage to not get locked into predefined associations for how to use these resources, we have all that is needed to be able to create our own options during challenging times.

KEY TAKE-AWAYS

▶ When reflecting on your resources, don't forget that everything can be a resource in a crisis. Start by looking at people, their skillsets, experience, knowledge, and potential, then the more materialistic things such as money and assets, as well as time and connections. Finally, look at subtle resources like motivation, creativity, and optimism. These latter components are most frequently overlooked but can be differentiators in a crisis.

▶ When faced with a critical situation, always assume that the resources you have at hand are the only ones you have access to, and remind yourself that what you have is all you need to succeed.

▶ Categorize your resources in a way that works for you, outlining their stock, whether you have unrestricted access to them or who owns them.

▶ Your resources are constantly changing, and it's important to regularly do an inventory. This way, you'll discover new ones while finding out which you're about to run out of and have lost already. Remember to be considerate with the ones that are in stock.

▶ Work on adopting a mindset that makes you regularly question how your resources can be used. Try to identify alternative ways that they could be put to use.

#3 PRACTICE HABITUAL READINESS

The day when I would finally be heading to Kabul, Afghanistan, was approaching, and I could feel myself becoming more excited, nervous, and anxious by the hour. I had spent the previous four months preparing for the moment when I was to enter a completely new and unknown world. I studied the culture, I had a great deal of training, I learned the basics of the main language, I watched films, I read books, and I talked to people who had been there before. When it was time to go, I couldn't wait to take off, and after a few long flights, I arrived in Kabul. Smelling the air for the first time, it was different. Hearing the unfamiliar sounds, it was different. The landscape of wonderful surrounding mountains and hills – it was different. Everything was different from what I had made it out to be, different from what I had prepared for it to be, and all of what I had studied suddenly felt meaningless. Yet, standing there on that airstrip for the first time, I understood that no matter how much longer I had prepared, nothing could have prepared me for this . . . and still, I don't think I could have been readier than in that moment.

THERE IS A PLAN, AND THERE IS REALITY

After people, or perhaps because of them, preparedness remains the holy grail of crisis management, but there is no ideal way to be best prepared for a future crisis. The generally accepted and most used approach to crisis preparedness is planning, and during my career, I also developed numerous crisis response plans, as well as risk mitigation and communication strategies for critical incidents. Our field is dominated by planning, risk assessments, analysis, and training; each has its value and its shortcomings. Then, in the middle of a debate a few years ago, I realised I hadn't once actually used any of these plans to actively respond to a crisis despite putting a lot of time and resources into their development. Reflecting on why this was the case, I realised it came down to a mix of relevance, complexity, practicality, assumptions, and experience. I explore some of them here, both in laying the foundation for an alternative approach and in the hope that sharing learnings and observations from my experience also assist practitioners who prefer to apply more traditional methods.

"Our plan is so far relevant until the first boots hit the ground." This phrase is frequently used by the military, and it's also relevant for crisis management plans. There's a plan, and then there's reality. The very foundation of planning is based on insights, experiences, and perspectives from previous crises that together form an assumption-based future scenario. We build these images for what could happen, which quickly turn into accepted screenplays. Yet, we need to maintain the awareness these are not facts or unmovable truths. In 2014, a series of earthquakes caused devastating destruction in and around Nepal's capital, Kathmandu. The international humanitarian community had been preparing for this scenario for years including planning and preparedness activities. A large amount of money was put into ensuring readiness for D-day and one would be right to assume the earthquake that eventually hit didn't come as a major surprise. Yet, it did to many. Moreso, when it happened, the situation turned into chaos very quickly, despite the many plans that had been developed to mitigate the chaos.

I was personally involved in the operation and experienced first-hand the limited effectiveness of plans. This isn't to say that nothing worked, but the outcome had little in common with what had been planned for. While the event had been anticipated, there were too many unknowns and an endless number of fixed assumptions. Responding organisations, agencies, and other actors had to adapt to the reality on the ground with few, if any, able to implement their original plans. To be clear, I'm not against planning. Among other uses, it can be of relevance in supporting staff less experienced in managing critical situations. However, I believe we should avoid becoming prisoners to our plans, as they quickly lose their significance and applicability when real-life crises turn out to have very little in common with the anticipated scenarios. If the real situation doesn't match our assumed version, it's best to let go of the plan. In its place, focus on the actual situation at hand, identifying problems and challenges faced in that present moment and reality.

NO PLAN WILL EVER BE COMPREHENSIVE

Whether it's the question of what will happen with the unaccompanied children that were evacuated from Afghanistan after the Taliban regained power or the disruption to fuel supply in the United Kingdom due to a shortage of drivers, no crisis management plan could have ever foreseen all of these situations. Crises occur within crises, making them like Russian Matryoshka dolls. Preparing for all of these eventualities is neither feasible nor realistic. The primary purpose behind crisis plans is to be able to handle the critical situation effectively and limit its negative impact. However, they can be neither sufficient nor comprehensive considering the complexity that accompanies crises. The dilemma that presents itself is readily observed: the more we want to include in a crisis plan, the more complex the plan becomes. On the other hand, if we keep it simple, we can't cater to the complexity of the situation. No matter how you turn it, there is no effective solution that covers both, which presents shortcomings and renders plans ineffective. This complexity is even more visible in large-scale crises. Different actors develop different plans, each from their point of view and with their interests in mind when a crisis evolves. These plans frequently prove to be competitive rather than complementary, thereby adding a level of difficulty instead of contributing to clarity in overall crisis management. Make peace with this and keep it in mind for yourself, your team, and your liaisons while working through critical times.

In addition, plans can also turn into limitations. For me, they are the biggest blockers of innovative solutions. In my discussions with different professionals involved in managing crises about their experiences working with plans, common comments have included finding them limiting, rigid, and impractical. There are, nevertheless, certain elements to plans that are more workable, if applied correctly. Such tools include standard operating procedures, checklists, and assessments. The former remains essential in air travel and industries that require triage protocols. There, they contribute to saving lives and reducing the likelihood of human error. However, checklists and protocols don't have the same relevance in all sectors that employ them. I worked frequently with checklists and so-called standard operating procedures and using them in a highly dynamic crisis lacks synchronicity and can feel artificial. There is hardly anything "standard" during a crisis and rigidity doesn't allow for a creative, tailored approach. Relying on a plan or standard approach too strictly limits openness to other potential options because some situations require us to react differently to all logic and knowledge. Remember that plans can lose their practicality due to the composition of a crisis team, the need to adapt the communication strategy as a result of new information, dilemma decisions, or other factors.

THE ASSUMPTION THAT THE PAST PREDICTS THE FUTURE

One day, I stood in front of my bookshelf, uninspired and looking for some challenging, thought-provoking pages that could fill my void of intellectual stimulation. I came across a book I had bought many years prior but had struggled reading at the time because I couldn't relate it to my experiences up to that point. The book was the international bestseller The Black Swan by Nassim Nicholas Taleb. Paraphrased and simplified, he underlines the fact that just because it has always been like this must not mislead us into thinking it will always be the same way. He outlines the now renowned example of the unexpected discovery of black swans overturning the long-standing reality and belief that all swans were white. The same is true for crisis preparedness, which continues to rely on assumptions about the future that build on past experiences. I once read it wasn't necessary to reinvent the wheel and that there is no crisis we haven't seen before, a statement with which I disagree because my own experience has shown me every crisis is unique even if triggers and characteristics can be similar. No two crises are the same.

Consider, for instance, the "forty-year crisis." I experienced it as did many of my friends and neighbours of the same age. We all had comparable symptoms and similar frustrations, yet each of us experienced their unique crisis. We were in different contexts, faced different decisions, and our solutions were also not alike. The same applies to large-scale crises. For example, the financial crisis in 2007–2008 and the one in 1929 had very little in common, besides the same label and some major dynamics.

Working on "the past predicts the future" principle in crisis management comes at high risk. As much as we can learn from the past, it will never help us predict the future. We might be able to predict that there will be another virus outbreak, another earthquake, or another market collapse, but this is where our ability to foresee future events ends. Many scientists and experts warned about the next global pandemic, though they were unable to predict when it was going to happen, where it would start and how it was going to evolve. We're not able to anticipate with full certainty when and where the next crises will hit us. Yet, it's not these unknowns that make us so vulnerable to crises, but the focus of trying to prepare for something about which we know nothing yet. There are natural limitations to this process, which we regularly cross in attempts to be prepared for what we don't know.

Crises need to be treated as unique scenarios, and the comparison with previous ones of a similar nature is to be performed with caution, or we end up in the assumption trap, where they change shape in our minds and become our reality. We work with assumptions in many areas of our lives, including getting ready for future events. However, I cannot overstate the importance of being aware when we base our thinking on assumptions. Awareness is what holds the key to effectively working with things we don't know for certain. Assumptions can easily be exposed and tested by exchanging perspectives with others – something that will also contribute to a reality check, a more comprehensive image of the situation, and new options.

EXPERIENCE CAN BE A DOUBLE-EDGED SWORD

"I have no idea. I just knew." At one point or another, most of us have answered similarly to a question, having felt what seemed to be a sixth sense. It's like an instinct – only it's not quite the same because this sense evolves with growing experience, as similar effects are true for almost everything we do because our experience and knowledge increase and automate some of our behaviour and actions. Once I had settled in Afghanistan and started to get used to the context, I noticed that some days I would leave the house and sense something was different. A feeling deep inside that was hard to describe, yet very real and impossible to miss. Something that triggered a reaction in me that I couldn't place but that, with time, I started to realise would repeatedly coincide with days when major security incidents were reported later. As I couldn't describe it, I reluctantly shared this sensation with my colleagues, and it turned out that I wasn't alone. In fact, several others reported a similar phenomenon. I started to explore this further and found that aid workers and professionals from other sectors who work in challenging environments have all reported similar sensations.

Gary Klein calls this tacit knowledge and describes it as the knowledge, skills, and abilities an individual gains through experience that is often difficult to put into words or otherwise communicate. This is highly relevant for crises, as it applies to both known and unknown situations, and I experienced this repeatedly when I was asked to develop a protocol for how to manage crises. I struggled because there were many things that I couldn't put into words – processes I couldn't describe because I just knew what to do. I reflected on what was preventing me from putting this down on paper while it seemed so clear when I was in the situation. Experience gives us more sources to draw from and helps us to assess and handle situations by virtue of comparison, but as described in my example, the challenge is the difficulty in using tacit knowledge for plans and procedures because experience is highly intuitive rather than standardised. Every crisis differs, and the advantage of applying tacit knowledge is in allowing us to adapt quickly to the situation and knowing where to place our focus. On the flip side, experience can also blind us. Imagine you're a seasoned driver and you have so much confidence and experience that you think you have attention available for other things, like writing a text message or making a phone call. These things, however, are misleading and frequently cause accidents resulting from an error of judgement or a simple slip of focus. Like anything else, experience is to be used with utmost caution.

A PRACTICAL MODEL: HABITUAL READINESS

What is the advantage and purpose of plans, then? Well, there are several, and it's all about reinventing their use.

Despite the aforementioned limitations in supporting a crisis response, plans have the underused advantage of being a great training and educational tool. They should be viewed and used as exercises and mini simulations based on the understanding of a reality that will constantly change. So, it's important to move away from preparing for something and simply get ready for anything. This allows us to fulfil our deep need for stability and control during a crisis. Plans can reveal subtle habits and gaps in the way an unforeseen or complicated event is being handled and the level of disruption it could cause. The key is to work with the scenario, independently focusing more on the elements of the plans that we can influence and less on possible risks of a potential scenario that we simply invent. Another way I use plans is to identify mental models, the strong assumptions that direct how I expect the response to a crisis should look. This enables me to become more aware of my assumptions and allows me to adapt or work with them.

I propose a shift of focus that comes with a change of terminology: let's stop talking about preparedness that lies in the assumption that there is something concrete for which to prepare. It's not about preparing for something but getting ready for anything. We cannot be prepared for something that we don't know, but we can be ready despite not knowing what's going to hit us. Some might say these concepts are one and the same, but in my experience, you can be prepared and have everything in place and yet, when the situation happens, you're not ready, so for me, it's all about developing readiness through positive habits. When preparing, we focus a lot on what might come about. As mentioned here, this isn't realistic when we talk about crises because, despite all of our ambitions of predicting how they will evolve, they all remain mere assumptions.

Readiness, for me, means focusing on our own abilities, resources, and competencies. It's not about getting ready for an event, such as an earthquake, a bank system collapse, or war. It means practising certain behaviour, developing habits, and focusing on building a strong foundation that isn't easily disrupted by a potential severe change. Our ambition must be the ability to continue working – ensured by a strong base from which to face turbulent times steadily and with control. It doesn't focus on the context but on the processes and behaviours. As opposed to preparedness, readiness must be nurtured and worked on constantly, and it consists of many subtle habits, all feeding into an overall concept. Changes are most effective when rooted in habits. Reflecting on my experience and considering the elements outlined above, I have identified eight core habits that are catalysts for fostering readiness. They are cornerstones of a crisis-resilient culture, and they present a practical model of reflection and action. By practising them regularly, you can lay a strong foundation and increase your readiness. I encourage you to be creative when it comes to implementing these habits, as they might seem obvious but should be adapted to the respective organisation or team.

Habit 1: Identify assumptions on a regular basis

Though sometimes necessary, assumptions are generally and overall dangerous. When working through crises, we work heavily with assumptions, and those who have worked with me irrespective of setting have most likely been driven insane by my constantly asking "Do we know, or do we just assume?" Being able to identify our own assumptions is a key skill in crisis situations. It helps us to determine whether we know something for a fact, or just think we do. This is a crucial denominator for our course of action. It might not be avoidable to work with assumptions. Nevertheless, it's important to reflect on them regularly and make it explicit when we do. This helps keep focus and control over our actions, increases awareness of blind spots, and leads to a more confident approach in finding solutions to problems during a crisis, thus aiding in the facilitation of reinvention.

Habit 2: Exchange perspectives regularly

We are all unique, and while we sometimes have overlapping experiences or use similar terms, we perceive them differently. Understanding and applying this fact is a decisive advantage in most areas of life. However, it's particularly effective during a crisis. The often-reported tunnel vision in stressful situations limits our perception, but it has its advantage, as it helps us focus. Sharing perspectives is one way of expanding that vision again while staying focused on the crisis. Exchanging perspectives leads to a more comprehensive understanding of the situation. It increases our options through the expansion of our zone of influence as well as our learning opportunities, both personally and collectively.

To be able to do this effortlessly and naturally in a crisis, it's essential to practice and make it a habit of exchanging and being open to perspectives. It's about creating an environment that facilitates the sharing of perceptions and experiences to avoid its introduction as a foreign concept during a crisis because this will only create insecurity. Accepting there is no one truth and that it consists of many different angles, it is powerful to practice reinvention and get ready for anything. I suggest making it a habit to exchange perspectives around all sorts of topics and projects.

Habit 3: (Re-)Focus on own scope of influence constantly

Managers and organisations are heavily influenced by the dynamics and contextual factors surrounding them in a crisis. To facilitate readiness, it's powerful to develop a way of regularly checking whether what we want to decide is within our scope of influence. The key here is to learn and identify ways that help us refocus on what we can influence. This way, we can proactively manage a crisis instead of passively responding to contextual developments. When in a crisis, this habit leads to a heightened sense of control and ability to act. An increased space to manoeuvre is a strong advantage when dealing with a crisis and allows for a more flexible approach to finding solutions.

Habit 4: Make space for emotions

Understanding emotions and how to work with them has become a core skill for success and, if done correctly, provides not only valuable information to the company and its management but ensures dedication, loyalty, and trust through wellbeing. This becomes even more important in crisis situations, where emotional reactions are common, unpredictable, and varied. It's essential to make space for emotions to be able to address the crisis holistically. It's been my experience that when addressed properly, emotions help to guide decisions, the development of ideas, and a more proactive way of dealing with a crisis. If not addressed, on the other hand, emotions tend to return at a later and often more inconvenient point in time, usually proving more intense and less controllable. Making space for emotions requires practice and creativity. When an organisation accepts and allows emotions and feelings and incorporates them into the workplace culture, it can facilitate a resilient culture because people will feel safer, more seen, and understood. Employees who can show up at work knowing their emotions are not dismissed and that there will be space for them at some point contribute to a strong and cohesive environment and ultimately a resilient culture.

Habit 5: Practice the magic moment

When I run workshops with teams and give them exercises that are under time pressure, almost all relate to the same trap: the illusion that speed equals effectiveness. I usually outline the task but then change one element or another. Being focused on completing the assignment within the timeframe, teams become paralyzed when faced with changing circumstances. This regularly creates confusion and slows adaptation. The key skill here is what I call the magic moment, a core habit for a crisis-resilient working culture and none other than calling a deliberate time-out. It means stopping everyone in their activities to get an overview and an understanding of the situation.

This pause provides an opportunity to practice all the aforementioned skills and actions to align the team and bring clarity to the situation. It presents the same opportunity to re-evaluate and readjust the process if so decided. The magic moment is a very effective tool that can be applied at any point in time and can be called by anyone. The illusion that taking breaks costs time is just that – an illusion. From experience and observation, I can tell you that teams who practice the magic moment are almost always more efficient, controlled, coordinated, and clearer in their responses. Plus, they are always more creative in their approaches. The most effective and successful teams that I have had the privilege to work with had one thing in common: they practised the magic moment regularly. Making a habit of this core catalyst will enable your organisation, team, and yourself to regularly ensure you control the situation, which is essential to responding effectively in a crisis.

Habit 6: Practice positive honesty at all levels

To be able to really change culture, shifting towards a reinventor's mindset, part of the cultural DNA is the practice of honesty. By honesty, I don't mean full and uncompromising transparency, as the aim isn't to overburden with details, while still giving an honest picture of the situation. Everything that's communicated is honest and factual, including identified assumptions being clearly communicated to everyone. The second key aspect of this habit is positivity. In a crisis, the sub-tone can make a decisive difference as to how the crisis is managed. In a little experiment outlined in the chapter on framing communication during crises, we tested the effect of framing facts more positively (whether implicitly or explicitly) yet avoiding sugar-coating them, and the difference in results was clear. The effect a simple reframe can have on how the honest situation is perceived is astounding and illustrates the hidden and unused potential that lies within this catalyst. A positive presentation of the honest situation can give an organisation a significant head-start in responding to a crisis and promote a more open and daring perspective amongst employees and leaders. As with all habits, it's essential that this habit is practised on all levels. This way, inclusion, ownership and determination are stimulated.

Habit 7: Implement insights continuously

Whether in organisations or in individuals, learning is frequently mistaken for acquiring information. The key to effective learning is to filter out the actual insights and, furthermore, find ways to make use of them for ourselves. Learning is about behaviour and behaviour often changes. The translation of insights into actions is something that tends to be ignored or underprioritised. Yet, being able to immediately apply what we have learned, thereby contributing to our development and progress, is the key to effective learning. We should, therefore, make it a habit to focus also on the implementation side of learning for it to be of use and contribute to readiness for critical times. To ensure this, start by clearly communicating insights and expectations including how to translate them into action enabling the creation of collective ownership over learning and making it a core part of your behaviour.

Habit 8: Transfer insights from other sectors

I have always been a fan and seen the benefits of learning across sectors. This is a strong element for facilitating real innovation and getting inspiration for how you can reinvent the use of resources. The old saying goes, when in Rome, do as the Romans do. However, if we all do what everyone else in our sector does, how can there be actual innovation? This becomes even more relevant in a crisis when all other stakeholders are also forced to make decisions. While a lot of things aren't directly transferrable, looking at other industries helps you get inspired and allows you to experiment with how some processes, tools, or approaches could work in your sector. Acquiring different approaches and tools and some new ideas gets us ready for when we must think differently. Doing this regularly turns the practice into a habit, and chances are that when a crisis comes, we'll be well prepared to either directly transform an idea from another sector or investigate another sector for ideas of how to manage this crisis proactively and through reinvention. Continuously looking into other sectors for insights is a cornerstone of a crisis-resilient culture.

For many years when asked why I worked in these contexts and how I prepared, I didn't have an answer. I couldn't articulate the "how," as I just felt ready. It was only through deep reflection that I came to understand this was possible through the habits I carried out subconsciously. We all possess such an ability, but most of us are generally unaware of its existence. Most habits offer instant gratification that leads to us continuing to do them. They're selected with the aim to create a behaviour that helps reduce the disruption that can be caused by the occurrence of a crisis. They can and should be performed irrespective of whether in crisis because they provide a foundation for development and reinvention and help to keep us calm, dealing with the problem in a dynamic ever-changing system.

KEY TAKE-AWAYS

▶ Every crisis is unique and must be treated as such. Comparisons between crises can lead to the assumption trap, whereby we assume that this is how the next crisis is going to look despite being unable to reliably predict as much.

▶ Plans regularly lose relevance when the crisis hits and either aren't comprehensive or workable. Plans have more relevance as simulation and training tools than a reliable way to respond to a crisis. Avoid relying too heavily on them.

▶ The aim of readiness is to build a state of mind, setup, and process that are necessary to avoid unexpected situations becoming disruptions and approach them through claiming ownership and designing reinvention.

▶ The most effective way to develop crisis readiness is through working with habits. The eight basic habits form the foundation. You can expand the set of habits relevant to your situation.

▶ Try to find creative ways to carry out your habits to stop them from becoming boring routines and make yourself even more adaptable in a crisis.

PART III
APPLICATION

#1 PROFILE
THE CRISIS SYSTEM

Many years ago, I worked for a large humanitarian organisation and was involved in the response to the famine that hit the Horn of Africa. The situation was neither unexpected nor lacking in warning signs. In fact, they'd already been apparent a year prior. However, despite strong physical evidence and research clearly indicating that conditions had turned critical with regards to shortages of food, water, and tense conflict in the area, large donors displayed limited interest in committing to funding for humanitarian support. Suddenly, the situation was declared a famine by the United Nations overnight, and all eyes were on us as one of the main actors to provide humanitarian assistance and handle the crisis. All key donors labelled it one of the worst humanitarian crises, and the situation demanded extensive funding and swift action. The balancing act was extremely complex and there were high risks involved, which turned it into a very sensitive operation. Due to external pressure, many immediate decisions had to be taken without sufficient understanding of the context and despite the clearly-stated threats. Additional risks also manifested along the way, and ultimately, the response faced many challenges despite being successful. The situation had been a crisis before the world acknowledged it as one, but the key stakeholders had to accept and ultimately label it a crisis for it to become a real focus that received the urgency it deserved and should have had long before.

THE MANY SIDES TO THE TERM CRISIS

In recent years, we have become too flippant, too liberal, and too inflammatory with the use of the word crisis. Language shapes the way we think and has an impact on how we approach situations, and the more recent use of the term has turned crisis into a constructed and dangerous label that is commonly used for situations that we all interpret differently, while the etymology of the word itself derives from the Greek krisis, translating to "decision point; choice; judgement." All considered, for me, the original meaning is still the most valid and best encompasses the elements all crises have in common: that decisions need to be made and once taken they are game-changers. More precisely, crises occur, when a fundamental systemic change is required; yet, the word alone lacks precision regarding what needs to change or is about change.

Crisis is a label that requires a multitude of perspectives to develop a comprehensive picture. Asking most people what they relate to the term crisis gets responses with overwhelmingly negative connotations. Due to these primarily negative biases, we involuntarily stand in our own way when it comes to dealing with challenging situations effectively. We might not see opportunities because we sit in the box that was labelled crisis and are blinded by our emotional response to it, a natural consequence of the term's general usage in a negative context, which despite all noble efforts, makes it difficult to reprogramme our biases towards such situations and see them as opportunities. In my early years in crisis management, I was also too busy trying to understand the ever-changing context to be able to see the situation as an opportunity. However, as you may have gathered if you've read this far, I've come to realise that we don't have to look at something as an opportunity for us to act as if it were one. What it does require is letting go of the label, accepting the situation for what it is, and avoiding judgement.

The psychology of communication explores the impact that words or phrases can have on our responses, reactions, wellbeing, and performance. For example, changing from "I have to" to "I want to" or "I choose to" increases the focus, commitment, and motivation to carry out a task by reclaiming control and ownership over our decisions. Positive wording and commitment also stimulate intrinsic motivation, helping to side-line negative biases we associate with crises and positively impacting the confidence of our decision-making as we move forward. Having spent my career in crisis management and managing situations that were labelled crises, I have learned to avoid using the term whenever I can and only call a situation a crisis if there is no other description for it. This might sound like a simplistic and inconsequential fixation on semantics, but I find it essential in shifting the focus and gaining control over unconscious reactions that lead to decisions and behaviours.

To achieve this, I use crisis profiling, a four-step process I have developed by fusing my experience in crisis management and systems conflict analysis with inspiration from the art and science of criminal profiling. The process helps a person to look at all of a situation's layers, dynamics, and characteristics, and it aims at giving a systemic picture of the circumstances at hand, providing you with an understanding of what's behind the "crisis" label, making the situation more workable and specific to your own challenges.

STEP 1: DECONSTRUCT THE FRAME

In 2016, while the headlines in Europe were dominated by the "refugee crisis," I coordinated a humanitarian response to Greece that included setting up a clinic for the provision of health services for displaced people from different conflict zones in Africa and the Middle East. In Norway, where I lived, headlines were also dominated by this "refugee crisis," even though it was experiencing a relatively low number of arrivals by comparison to central

European countries. While I also occasionally used the term in my role, I always struggled to pinpoint its actual meaning when doing so. I didn't see the term as having any relevance where I lived, and the label only brought about further stigma and divisions. Crisis is frequently used as an umbrella term, which lacks specificity and can often be rhetorically dangerous as well as a hindrance to providing comprehensive and effective crisis management. I use two lenses to help its deconstruction and develop a more nuanced understanding of the situation in front of me:

Lense A: Being aware of the simplicity paradox

One of the key elements for effective crisis management is to clearly define the crisis, which means being able to name your problem and the decisions at hand. Ironically, using the term crisis gives a false sense of simplicity, thereby undermining the systemic complexity the situation and decision-making entail. Hearing, reading, or talking about a crisis triggers associations at our cognitive and emotional level, indicating a sense of seriousness as well as a call to action. It can create an erroneous reference point for decision-makers, as was the case with the refugee crisis, making it more difficult for stakeholders to identify the actual problem. This leaves room for interpretation for what this urgency relates to and ends up being too vague for us to be able to identify what needs focus and attention.

What I refer to as the simplicity paradox makes it difficult to deal with a crisis and contributes to uncertainty because it leaves stakeholders in a position where they're forced to pick and choose the measures that are to be taken and the choices that ought to be made. I faced this challenge many times in my career. While I found simple crisis labels somewhat liberating, I regularly experienced a struggle to focus on where to start managing the situation. As a crisis manager, it wasn't only the expectation that I handle the crisis, but I frequently had to do so in the spotlight while my actions were being scrutinized. As a result, I was often tempted to produce fast wins in what might have been a subconscious effort to save face and secure my own position. I opted to solve the easy problems first but ultimately found that quick successes were almost always more for show than of substance in making a difference to the overall situation.

Like placing a band-aid on a wound that hasn't been disinfected, underneath the situation will get worse, and the problems that need attention will only grow. The tough choices not only remain, but they have a habit of increasing in pressure and urgency. Therefore, to be able to define the most urgent problems at hand, the "crisis" umbrella needs to be refined and dissected with a focus on the different critical situations connected to and impacted by it. It might not be possible to address all issues at hand, but the unpacking gives an overview of all the different angles the crisis can be worked on, all of which combined make for effective crisis management. Dissecting what lies beyond the frame opens the frame for prioritization, honest dialogue, effective use of resources, and timely decision-making.

Lense B: Discovering the attributional misconception
Without a doubt, "Europe Hit by Refugee Crisis" makes for a catchier headline than "Crisis in Europe." We hardly see headlines like the latter because the word crisis alone is too vast a description that gives us insufficient information. While using the frame crisis gets minds wondering, we need something to which to connect our alertness because every crisis happens within a context and is related to different factors. To specify the situation, we add these explanatory attributions related to the crisis, such as inequality crisis, unemployment crisis, or skills crisis. These add-ons are intended to

explain what the situation is about; however, they present symptoms, effects, or triggers of the crisis in a simplified way rather than the core issue that needs to be addressed and managed.

Refugee crisis is an overall label for a challenging situation that was largely triggered by an increased population movement stemming from core issues that include decades of conflict, war, persecution, as well as political and economic instability, to name a few. What might make for a practical, simple, easy, and relatable frame carries the challenge that refugees are held responsible for the burden that originated in other parts of the system. The title paved the way to the misinterpretation that refugees and migrants coming to Europe were the actual problem, while the core issues might have been a lack of willingness, mechanisms, and agreements to cooperate among and between European states, or the neglect to support peace processes in the war-torn countries of origin. This umbrella term had an additional negative effect due to the further stigma and prejudice it placed on refugees being responsible for the crisis.

Attributions are a good way to specify the topic related to the crisis, but there is a real danger that the attribute becomes the mental image of what needs to be dealt with and handled. While this might be implicitly applicable for some crises, it's essential to reflect whether the attribute correctly captures the issue or if more explanation is needed. When I started writing this book, the UK was hit by a "job crisis" – at least according to headlines. The issue that required addressing seemed to be "jobs"; however, the label itself neither gives any specific information on the actual problem nor helpful details regarding the situation. What are the systemic issues that make this a job crisis? What needs to be solved? And has it become a job crisis because of another crisis? These are just a few potential considerations that would need to be clarified.

The answers to the above and more questions would provide a better understanding, but sometimes they are neither unpacked nor discussed openly. Consequently, when used in public debate, different people interpret different things and add issues to the narrative they relate to the situation. This results in a misconception of what is the actual crisis, adding complexity rather than providing clarity. It is also why I place a great emphasis on getting to the heart of the contributing factors rather than focusing on the symptoms of a crisis. Furthermore, these frames can also serve and be used as an opportunistic tool to divert decision-makers' attention from the actual crisis by dealing with simple and fast decisions first, which can be communicated as measures to resolve the crisis.

A simple and catchy umbrella term is highly effective when framing the situation to dictate a public narrative. While it doesn't capture the complexity, it ensures the public remembers and talks about it, giving a leader the opportunity to justify crisis measures. A simple and broad label allows for any measure to be argued and adopted as a crisis management tool while the simplicity allows for a qualitative assessment of whether the measures were effective and contributed to managing the crisis. In some instances, this blindness to the core issues is deliberately used by leaders as a form of communication to protect and reduce the pressure on themselves. While this approach helps to potentially evade accountability when bringing additional issues into the debate at a later stage, it can lead to criticism about why these measures weren't raised earlier.

Ultimately, being too focused on the main topic invites the risk of other important aspects being ignored, which happens frequently. In some cases, a crisis increases in complexity after the first decisions are taken, which leads to a multi-dimensional crisis rather than a situation where certain areas need attention and action. While focusing on one topic in the labelling has significant advantages with regard to communication and immediate focus control, it can put one in danger of losing control over the narrative. A one-topic crisis can create unintended blindness to rapid context transformations and might have only limited overlap with its initial label. For these reasons, I have made it a habit to clearly define the crisis being faced to specify the issue at hand, create a common reality of what is needed for an effective response, and ensure I focus on the essential decisions.

STEP 2: MAP THE SYSTEM DYNAMICS

When I was first introduced to systems thinking through its application in conflict analysis, it quickly filled a gap connected to how we try to understand complex situations. Systems thinking is the balancing act of looking at everything as a system, where factors influence each other, and dynamics that lead to a very energetic and changing web of loops and interactions. I was immediately intrigued by this type of thinking because it helped me to illustrate a more vibrant and comprehensive image of different situations contributing to more clarity. I frequently observed these dynamics in crises. The term alone throws us off balance by creating a false sense of urgency, thereby triggering several premature reactions. In turn, their consequences trigger the need to react further, and this often turns into a dynamic and increasingly unpredictable spiral; a consequence of decisions taken based solely on a focus that is too narrow.

To map the dynamics of a system around a crisis, we must consider all the factors identified in the first step, when deconstructing the label.

This should have ideally revealed several elements that are affected and interconnected, thereby feeding into the crisis. It's crucial to identify so-called loops, which are factors that keep reinforcing each other. Not identifying this can lead to overlooking essential information when managing a crisis, which results in ineffective decisions. The most common example is the Cold War, where the USA perceived the proliferation of Russia as a threat and reacted with proliferation on their end, which was perceived as a threat by Russia in return and led to more proliferation by them and so on.

I fell victim to this oversight many times in my early career, leading me to always feel like I was dealing with a crisis passively and reactively, never able to get into balance. Over time, I started to understand that no decision is made in a void. Moreover, the situations I was confronted with were complex and included different actors, layers, and dynamics. To understand a crisis, I try to understand the context in which it is unfolding, as well as map characteristics, dynamics, and elements it consists of with the aim of getting as complete a picture as possible before deciding what to do next. I apply systems thinking in crisis by attributing them personalities and referring to individual characteristics that they show. Some crises appear quite suddenly and require fast decisions, while others are developing slowly and allow for a more considered approach. Some crises are influenced by a constantly changing context, while others happen in a rather predictable environment. Also, some concern a few people while others concern many. Across the board, once a situation is labelled a crises, it tends to develop a life of its own. Understanding the dynamics of what works for and against it are important to understand and map out as a means to specify your options.

STEP 3: ANALYZE THE POWER PLAYERS

The example of famine in the Horn of Africa also illustrates another challenge with the term crisis: it carries a different weight, depending on who introduces and uses the term. I frequently outline that I think a crisis is acted upon only when the stakeholders and decision-makers acknowledge it as such. There are both advantages and dangers in labelling a situation a crisis, and it's essential to keep these in mind when you profile your own crisis. In the situation above, the positive element was that it forced stakeholders to act and make decisions, which is necessary during crises. The downside was that it had felt like a crisis for the affected people – who remained unheard when calling for support – long before it was labelled one. Keeping this in mind will help you to understand why the label might be used and what traps to avoid when working with it yourself.

Considering all this, I always ask the question, "Who owns the crisis?" The ability to influence this perception illustrates that a crisis is something declared out of a power position. In practice, I repeatedly observe a gap between the parties managing the crisis and those most affected by it. The power to declare a crisis does not lie with everyone in this triangle. To understand and get an overview about who plays which role and how the dynamics show themselves, it's important to assign roles in the crisis at hand to certain people or groups. This is also essential to potentially identify a strategic use of the term crisis, if some actors have a specific interest to do so, which in turn influences the decision-making. The most effective and sustainable way to manage a crisis lies within the overlap of the three groups.

Interestingly, the role of being a stakeholder is constantly changing with the problem that is being solved. While someone can declare a crisis, not everybody will necessarily be concerned by it at that moment. However, the constant decision-making, reactions and actions change the context and thereby the roles. Logistics companies might not have considered the refugee crisis a crisis for them at its onset, yet a year later while simultaneously facing partially closed borders between European countries for their normal services, they found themselves amid it when people were discovered hidden in freight and haulage trucks to transport them across borders. A crisis consists of a fluid web of actors where roles are in a constant state of flux. As such, it's essential to regularly map out these actors and stakeholders along with their interests and actions, as it allows us to monitor changes that can have a substantial effect on our own situation.

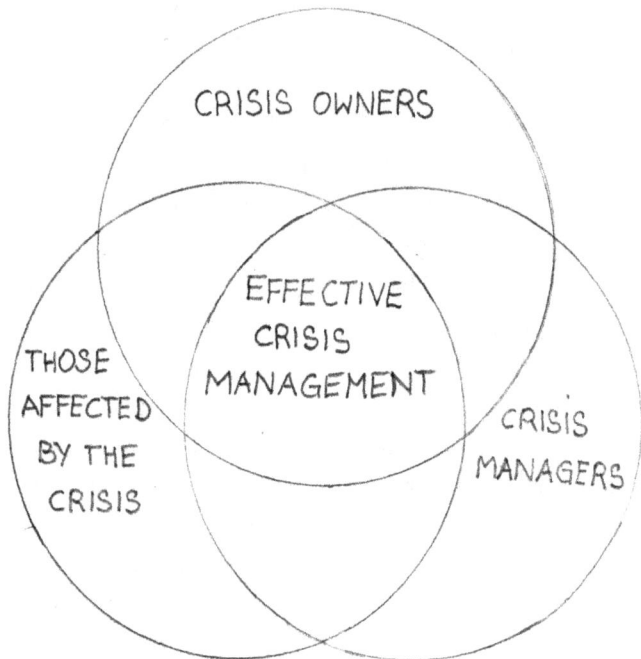

Figure 4 – Effective Crisis Management Sphere

Step 4: Identify and specify your crises

Once you've worked through the system and developed an understanding of the dynamics and the people involved, it's essential to look at yourself.

The reason why this is so important is that it's the part of the analysis where you can identify your core challenges and thereby what crisis you're facing. While it's technically possible, I never experienced that a crisis consists of just one key decision. There are always several choices to make. Understanding what turns the situation into a crisis for you helps you to specify the choices you are facing and potentially will be faced with. Such an overview presents a good starting point, but it is nevertheless important to remember that some of the future choices are not yet visible or might present themselves only as consequences of decisions that other stakeholders make. The easiest way is to not start with the most obvious decision but map the spectrum of key decisions. To make this selection workable, it is helpful to define prioritization criteria to identify the most urgent ones. This should allow you to have a starting point, but it's crucial to regularly repeat this process and reflect on whether there are new decisions that should be prioritised. This simple process also allows me to keep my focus on managing my crisis or realise that I might not be affected by the crisis anymore, thus allowing me to step out of the crisis frame.

One way to test the relevance of the identified decisions is to revert them back to the overall context. I regularly check how our decisions connect to the crisis and how they influence the development of the system. Remember that some decisions have more impact than others, and not all decisions show immediate effects. In addition, acknowledge how the crisis makes you feel and how it affects you. Have regular exchanges where emotions find space, are acknowledged and dealt with. It's unrealistic and unwise to try to ignore that the label crisis alone can trigger emotions in us. In turn, however, these emotions can help us better understand the crisis at hand and the decisions to be made, as they strongly indicate whether or not we're getting closer to what's missing during a crisis. Lastly, when working with deconstructing the crisis label, there are also a few common pitfalls important to keep in mind:

Pitfall 1: Stability illusion

Every system has the core aim of keeping itself alive, and in a crisis, we often unwillingly contribute with resistance to inevitable change. I frequently observe that we allocate a lot of resources to maintaining the situation as it was before due to a stability illusion, while this is almost always the reason why we are facing a crisis, thus presenting the opportunity to rework the system and turn it into something new. I elaborated on this element in the chapter on reinvention.

Pitfall 2: Crisis contagion

We are social animals, and our ability to emotionally connect with other people and empathise with their situations and experiences also has evident downsides. One of them is that we easily adopt emotional states from other people without noticing it. This well-researched phenomenon is called social contagion. When listening to someone talking about their crisis, it's essential to observe our own emotional state. It's not unlikely that we experience similar emotional responses, thereby compromising our outside perspective and the ability to provide support without being affected.

Pitfall 3: Post-decision relaxation

Crises are quite intense and can be energy-draining. It can be tempting to relax and take a break, particularly in situations when we have worked a long time to find a solution and finally made a choice following a lot of intense hours, worries and contemplation. These periods, unless they are proper rest for self-care, must be approached like afternoon naps, not too long and not too far away from the situation because it happens easily that the focus shifts and we think the worst is over. If the crisis is ongoing, we must maintain a level of readiness because if alertness drops too low, it becomes very difficult to get to a high-performance level again.

Throughout my career, I have come to understand that not everything with the label crisis is a crisis and that some situations that deserve to be named a crisis never get the label. I find the term dangerously underestimated in its ability to affect us and our wellbeing, as well as how we deal with a situation. I've noted that the term is more commonly used as a matter of convenience to influence a situation and create momentum, while it doesn't carry much content in and of itself. I generally avoid using the term because, in many situations, it comes with a lot of weight that shifts an easily manageable situation to a suddenly challenging one. More often than not, the problem doesn't lie in the crisis itself but in the system that is shaken in leading up to it. When coming across the term, I recommend you look behind the frame, the players involved in using the term, and the respective context.

KEY TAKE-AWAYS

▶ Crises are undefined individual mental frames that we fill with our associations and perceptions. The attributes that they are given are often simplified and misleading. For this reason, it's essential to deconstruct the frame and find out the details behind the label.

▶ Crises are periods where systems are being challenged, as they need to be significantly altered or overthrown. It's important to map out and understand the system being challenged if one hopes to manage it effectively.

▶ Every crisis is dominated by power players and stakeholders, some of which might be actively working to keep a crisis or the crisis narrative alive. It's important to identify the different stakes and interests in a crisis.

▶ Not every crisis is everyone's crisis. Regularly consider whether you are concerned by the crisis at hand and how it affects you. To define your problem, it's important to try to formulate it in a way that ensures you have ownership over it.

▶ There are common pitfalls that work actively against effective crisis management. Try to adopt a way to regularly check whether you've stepped into them.

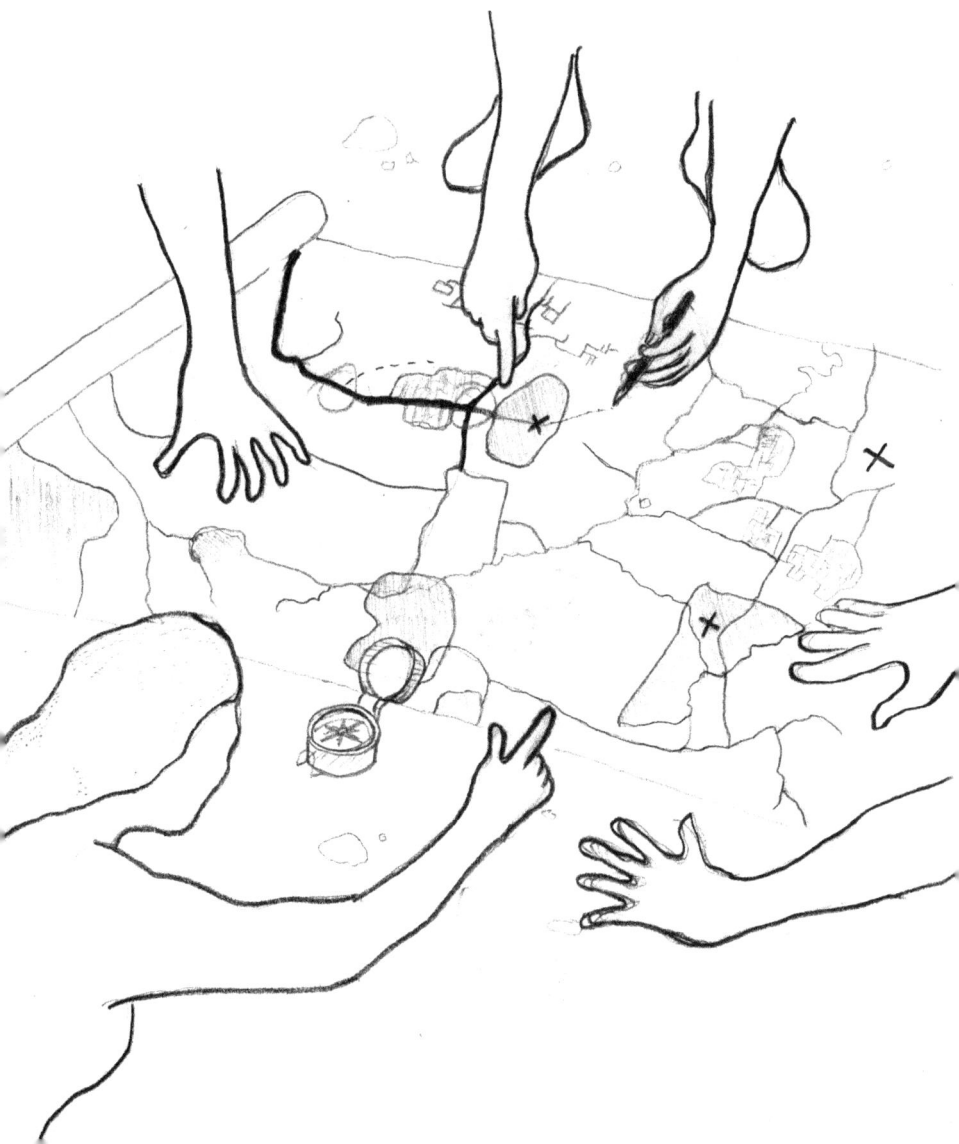

#2 EXPAND
YOUR OPTIONS

Many years ago, I was sent on short notice to a country experiencing the early stages of civil unrest. In what later turned into a long-lasting and devastating conflict, my task was to support the team on the ground in preparing to continue our work if a long and bloody conflict were, indeed, to materialise. From the moment I set foot in the country, I was under surveillance by entities that didn't even try to hide it. There was a clear interest in what I was doing in the country, which escalated from observation to intimidation. There were near-daily break-ins to my hotel room, whereby documents and my camera equipment were stolen and the room was left in a state like those seen in movies. My phone was tapped, and I was regularly cut off during calls. It worked, and I became increasingly wary and suspicious of who to trust. I was dependent on working with people on their readiness but became increasingly insecure about their motives and loyalty. I felt my work was significantly impacted and that my options to carry out successfully what I was tasked to do were impacted by the context and stakeholder interference. I knew that one wrong move could compromise the operation in the whole country. I was left with little leverage, and the situation required me to refocus on what I could control. I started not taking my phone with me anymore; I stopped documenting conversations on paper, electing to memorise them instead; I tested how the information would spread by deliberately adding different details in conversations with certain colleagues. Slowly, step by step, I started to regain some leverage and carried out my assignment, achieving the desired results.

FOCUS ON YOUR SCOPE OF LEVERAGE

"Keep your focus" used to be my standard response when asked about the most important thing to remember when we're faced with a crisis. However, in recent years, this felt increasingly insufficient, as it missed the element of what to focus on. I found my answer while running a workshop with a group of young emerging leaders, who were discussing that it seemed impossible to know where to start when managing a crisis. When they asked me where I would start, I instinctively replied, "By finding out what I can influence." Why? Because the single-most important thing to remember when dealing with the unknown is to focus on your scope of leverage.

TAKING BACK THE DRIVER'S SEAT – EXPLORE THE "FEELING" AND EMOTION OF LOSING CONTROL

We struggle when situations become overwhelming, our plans fail, too much information is coming in, everyone seems to want something from us, or we feel like control is slipping through our fingers. It becomes difficult to keep an overview of the situation, and it seems impossible to know what to prioritise. I experienced all of these difficulties at one point or another in almost every crisis I worked through, where whatever I did felt like I could only react and left me a step behind, leading me to feel like I was about to lose control. When I've asked other people dealing with a crisis how they feel, I have heard this or similar descriptions, which has empowered me with the knowledge and acceptance that this sensation is very common, totally normal, and likely essential.

Though I know full well this isn't as easy as it sounds, it took me many years to understand there is absolutely no shame in accepting that we feel like we're losing control. On the contrary, I discovered it to be a perfect starting point for managing a crisis effectively. These reactions are normal and shouldn't be dismissed, ignored, or controlled by rational thinking. Emotions and emotional reactions must be given their space because you can only move on to less emotionally charged actions once they're dealt with. This isn't an easy and straightforward process, as it requires a high level of honest self-insight and the ability to self-reflect. External perspectives are extremely helpful here too, as they present the opportunity to reality-check what we experience. When we have emotional reactions to situations, our inner compass is giving us an indication about what we're reacting to. As a result of our lingual development, we increasingly use the word feeling in connection with triggers, thereby creating the illusion of a feeling. These reactions, however, usually aren't categorised as feelings yet because this would require reflection and active exploration. To refocus, we must go deeper and explore the actual emotion and the feeling beyond it.

During the phase of emotional influx, it's common to focus on elements outside ourselves. This starts with blaming others for our situation and potentially peaks with the negativity lens that the universe must have conspired against us because only bad things happen to us. Through this mindset, we hand over ownership of our fate to others and end up in a reactive role to changes occurring around us. Emotions must have their space but not only in the form of ranting negativity. When the first strongly-charged emotional responses start to become less intense, the moment begins to open to redirect focus. To be able to use our emotions to our advantage, we must identify the core triggers that help us take back control in the uncertainty of the dynamic situation. To talk about control in dealing with uncertainty might seem like a paradox, but the aim isn't to control uncertainty; it's to control what we can control, re-focusing on our own scope of influence instead of what the dauntingly unknown context keeps throwing our way. To get ahead of a crisis and create a feeling of control, it's essential to remind yourself of what lies within our zone of leverage. Therefore, we must start by understanding and accepting our limitations, followed by a shift in focus to what we can change and control.

ZONE OF LEVERAGE – A FLUID CONCEPT

So, what is a zone of leverage and why bother with it? I define it as a fluid space where we can implement our actions independently from others, and it has four factors that influence its expansion and reduction: autonomy, ability, certainty and dynamic.

Autonomy – This element determines the extent to which we have responsibility and independence over our decisions or need to rely on others. It connects to ownership as explored in different chapters of this book. We might be able to influence things, but the control still lies with someone else. Despite being so obvious, this detail is frequently overlooked when it comes to dealing with crises, thus causing severe difficulties.

Ability – Ability encompasses elements such as knowledge, competence, and the resources we need to realise an idea and plan.

Certainty – Certainty can be achieved by identifying and testing our assumptions and mental models (the strong and deep-rooted understanding of how things are supposed to work). If we're uncertain about something, using it as the foundation for our potential options moving forward makes us vulnerable.

Dynamic – The space representing our zone of leverage is dynamic because the creation of different options can expand or reduce it. Similarly, it's impacted by the context as well as actions and decisions others make.

When working with this concept, I illustrate how strongly our zone of leverage is connected to our perception. It's easy to misjudge it by over- or underestimating what we can control, thereby wasting resources or missing out on opportunities. There are four dimensions that define the space:

Accurate: The awareness and perception of how autonomous actions can be taken and how aligned, realistic, and matched they are to our own ability is the (dynamic) actual zone of leverage. In this segment, the scope is labelled dynamic because you have influence over expanding and reducing it. You have the possibility to expand your scope of influence and increase your control over the crisis by testing assumptions and new perspectives while creating your own innovative options based on your resources.

Inflated: If we falsely assume that we have autonomy or the ability to implement a choice, we have an inflated perception of what we can control and an inflated zone of leverage.

Deflated: Failed attempts and long-lasting crises can lead to our feeling overwhelmed and unable to control the situation. In turn, this leads to underestimating and doubting our own ability and autonomy, causing a perception of our scope of control being smaller than it is and a deflated zone of leverage.

Outside: If we realise that we can neither decide and act independently nor have any certainty to realise our preferred choice, we're outside the zone of leverage.

This model helps me to identify blind spots and vulnerabilities when I manage a critical and uncertain situation. It also helps decision-making, as it aids in identifying what I can influence. I take a starting point in the aforementioned definition of scope of control, ask questions centred upon autonomy and ability, and try to plot ideas, measures, and actions into the respective zones, allowing me to choose what to focus on.

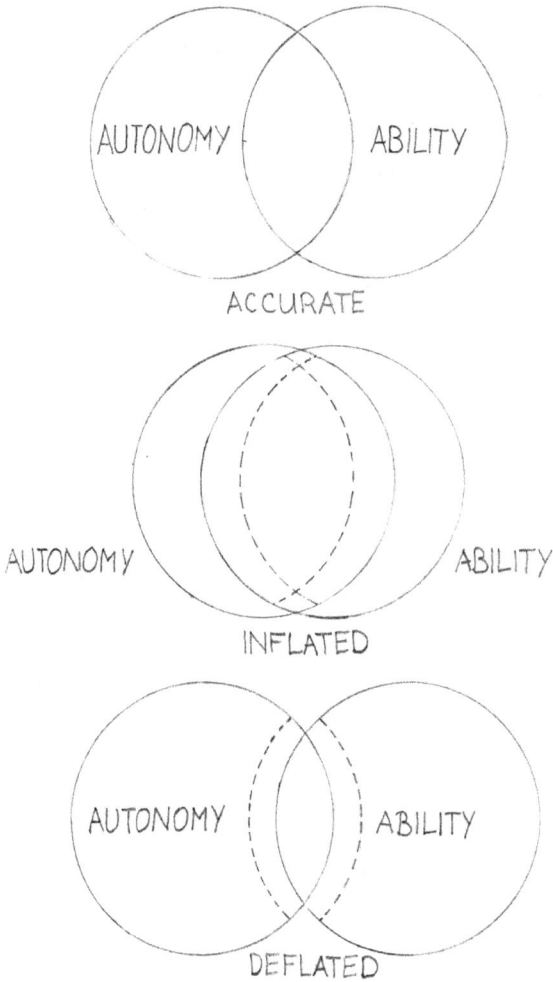

Figure 5 – Zone of Leverage / Dimensions

HOW TO IDENTIFY AND EXPAND
YOUR ZONE OF LEVERAGE

The zone increases and decreases permanently as decisions are being taken from different stakeholders. With our scope of control being a fluid concept, we can impact its boundaries and expand, maintain, or reduce it as we see fit. It might seem illogical to reduce the scope of control deliberately, but in some cases, too many options can lead to a paralysing effect and block us from focusing. Then, it makes sense to reduce the zone to have fewer options. This facilitates prioritisation. Maintaining and expanding what we can control, on the other hand, is harder and requires active work, the right mindset, and determination. During my work as a crisis manager, I started using habits that help me keep focus and influence on my zone of leverage:

Habit 1: Look for leverage points
How we react and respond to changes in the context impacts us in return. This dynamic interdependency is what makes crises so unpredictable. Applying systematic thinking allows me to understand the factors and dynamics influenced by my decision and helps to identify leverage points where we can have an impact. Leverage points are also where we find our zone of control. Naturally, all elements in a system have an influence on it, and by adopting a systemic view, you can work out where your leverage points are and deduce options to expand your zone of leverage to address them.

Habit 2: Define the relevant problem
One of the most common pitfalls I see is the lack of specification of the actual problem at hand. This is crucial, as it sets the tone and allows you to create options that are relevant to your actual problem and not be too vague and end up with choices that don't present

relatable solutions. A rule of thumb that I adopt when working with problem statements is that they are formulated as a question and are made from my position. An example would be: "The problem is that there is bad weather predicted for the day I have my birthday party." An alternative could be: "What can we do, despite the weather predictions?" You immediately regain not only the room for manoeuvre but reclaim the responsibility, an automatic first step towards taking control.

Habit 3: Find an anchor

I've referenced the importance of anchoring before. From my own experience in uncertain situations, the lack of an anchor, of something that can give you direction in seemingly constant change around you can cause or exacerbate this feeling of uncertainty. I have learned that having such an anchor that grounds you can be a real differentiator in a crisis. These anchors are all around us. They can be a catchphrase that we repeat to ourselves or within our team if the situation gets overwhelming; an inside joke that takes out the seriousness and lightens the mood, which can make all the difference; something that you carry in your pocket; a song that you like to listen to; or even a person that you like to talk to.

Habit 4: Use the power of disruption

You might have observed that when people face critical situations, sometimes they can drift into a manic and hysteric state, which makes it difficult to establish contact with them. Other times, they're completely paralysed and unable to think or act at all. These are modern versions of our fight, flight, freeze response, and innate behaviours to ensure our survival. These are instinctive, difficult to predict in their occurrence, and limit our zone of leverage. What is useful to snap us out of these situations is a slight form of shock, something unexpected but safe that disrupts the behaviour pattern.

The function of this action is mainly to distract from the context and the crisis itself. This mental break allows you or someone else to refocus, take a step back, and take a break. This brief moment interrupts our thought patterns and helps us regain ownership of the situation and our own actions and decisions.

Habit 5: Practice the magic moment
There are a few things that reoccur in this book, and one of them is a reference to what I call the magic moment. It's a simple practice, where you take pause and stop for a second to get an understanding of everything that's happening – a chance to regain an overview of all that needs to be done. I repeatedly fell into the same trap of being encouraged to perform, solve, and handle a task, but jumping straight into action mode can lead to oversights and a lack of understanding of other important elements to the context, creating a disconnect between the situation, how it affects us, and our range of options. Pausing allows for quick and regular check-ins to ensure the understanding of the context, priorities, and next steps are aligned, and it also allows space for reflection over our assumptions about our leverage points and abilities.

Habit 6: Accept our limitations
A natural reaction to feeling helpless is to overcompensate and work even harder, sleep less, and put more energy into solving the problem. This often-subconscious approach can quickly turn into a toxic pendulum that swings between helplessness and failure due to the misconception of our ability. As mentioned earlier, it's important to understand the real limitations of your zone of control. Moreover, we need to accept if there are things over which we have no control. This requires honesty and the awareness of our own limitations. It's extremely helpful to include perspectives from others when working on this because we tend to have biases due to our own

work, emotions, and other factors that can influence our perceptions. Accepting our limitations prevents us from wasting resources and instead redirects the attention to creating and implementing ideas. An easy way of doing so is by simply and repeatedly asking yourself the question: Is there anything I can do about this situation? If the answer is "no," you repeat the process until you get to a point where the answer is "yes!" If you get a repeated "no," this can also help with the realisation that you have no control and that your focus should be elsewhere.

While not all situations are so serious as my opening example, many crises share a feeling of overwhelm and a point when it feels like everything is out of control. This is a very normal phenomenon and in many ways the nature of a crisis. The art is in being a step ahead and remembering there is always something over which we have control, however small. I've learned to not give up before I've found the things that I can control and taken them as a starting point for expanding my options. In the vacuum where the new situation takes shape – and this happens throughout the process of all decision-making – I work on being at the forefront in shaping it through my actions. Instead of waiting passively for options to present themselves, I develop and expand my own leverage, thereby taking ownership and control over the situation.

KEY TAKE-AWAYS

▶ Control and leverage in an uncertain context might seem like a paradox, but there is always something we can control and have influence over. It's important to regularly refocus on these elements as a starting point. They provide stability and an anchor before starting to expand the options available.

▶ The zone of leverage is an ever-fluid concept that's influenced by other stakeholders' decisions as well as your own. Combined with your changing resources and shifting power dynamics, this causes an unpredictable context.

▶ The zone of leverage is affected by the following factors: autonomy, ability, certainty, and dynamic.

▶ When expanding your options use your resources and remember to focus on the ones you have full access to and ownership of; otherwise, your leverage is prone to assumptions and illusion and your crisis management approach will be undermined.

▶ In some cases, it's wise to reduce your own zone of leverage and limit your options. Too many choices can lead to the paradox that decisions become more difficult to make.

#3 MAKE CONFIDENT DECISIONS

Many years ago, when in the eastern provinces of the Democratic Republic of Congo (DRC) for work, I travelled with Jean (name changed), a driver from Burundi, who was visiting the country for the first time. This part of the world has been a war zone, especially along ethnic lines, for decades. While I couldn't relate to what Jean must have been feeling, I could sense that he was permanently on alert in this foreign yet strangely familiar context for him. One afternoon, while we were in town so I could pick up money, I jumped back in the car and Jean started driving before I was able to put on my seatbelt, and we were immediately stopped by an armed policeman who demanded an outrageously high fine because I wasn't wearing one. I decided to pretend I didn't speak French, thinking it would be smartest to get out of the situation by making communication difficult. However, my idea didn't work very well because I had left Jean to negotiate with the officer, something which was potentially very explosive in the context given their respective backgrounds and origins. To my shock, Jean then tried to play his own escape strategy, claiming that we worked for an influential organisation in the region, which wasn't the case. I found myself in a situation where I had to decide whether to reveal that I spoke French and admit to my lying to the already agitated policeman or risk Jean getting into even more trouble for also lying himself. As the policeman started to walk around the car, I suddenly heard the back door open and realised that Jean hadn't had a chance to lock it as is standard in conflict contexts. The next thing I heard from the backseat was: "Take me to your office."

NO ACTION, NO DECISION

Decisions are unavoidable in a crisis, and during my work, I've been faced with countless challenging ones. Since then, I've spent much time reflecting on them and learning from my behaviour, mindset, and considerations. In this chapter, I outline some key insight from my own experience and delve into why being confident when making decisions in a crisis is the single-most-important quality stakeholders must have to manage a critical situation to the best of their abilities. I also explore how the aspects discussed in previous chapters play into this. We generally refer to mental processes as decisions. However, I argue that simply stating what we are planning to do something makes it a choice, an intent, or an ambition. It only becomes a decision when we act upon it. During emergency operations, I made it a habit to never communicate a decision before we knew that we could also implement it. This is a result of two considerations in decision-making:

A. Who owns the decision?
B. Can it be implemented and realised?

Some decisions might not be fully owned by the one or ones making them because to implement a decision, they need to rely on other actors or the availability of resources. In my very early days in humanitarian assistance, I was tasked with conducting a needs assessment of the Pygmies in the eastern provinces of the Democratic Republic of Congo. A field visit was originally discussed, but the final decision lay with me based on whether I could organise logistics in the region. When the time came and I had established a network, I informed the organisation about my decision to travel to the region, but I was informed in turn that they would not be willing to fully fund the trip – something which I hadn't anticipated. While I had informed my network on the ground about my decision, I learned I wasn't the one who ultimately owned it, and the trip, to their and my own disappointment, didn't happen.

141

Similar scenarios could be observed in some of the world's biggest football clubs during the COVID-19 pandemic. These clubs with the best players in the world on contract, paying the largest salaries suffered substantial financial losses due to lockdowns and subsequent restrictions. In many cases, they had no solutions. Several of their executives announced the decision to cut player salaries in order to cut expenses; however, when they tried to put this decision into effect, they faced resistance from the players and their union. Given that not all stakeholders were on board made the decision difficult to realise and ultimately obsolete because no agreements could be reached. However, the primary stakeholders were still responsible for announcing the decision, so they were the ones held accountable for why it wasn't implemented.

These situations can be avoided by making the possibility and clarity of how to realise the choice a key focus of discussion and deliberation before taking the decision. These two considerations – ownership and implementation – are particularly important during a crisis because they affect everyone and can cost a lot of resources, including time, if the implementation aspect of a decision isn't considered sufficiently or doesn't materialise. To make decisions you need to consider both the ownership of the actual choice and the realisation of its implementation. This fine distinction and ability to implement your decisions also has an impact on your perception as a stakeholder and the trust that you receive from other stakeholders.

THE IMPORTANCE OF CONFIDENCE AND CONVICTION

"If I had to make this decision again knowing what I know now, I would make a different choice." While the aim of this commonly used phrase is to illustrate the ability to learn and reflect, it can

signal a lack of confidence and conviction in one's own decisions. Throughout my experience of working in complex situations, I learned that the key elements to decision-making are confidence and conviction. They won't only allow you to make seemingly impossible choices but will also help you to avoid feelings of regret and remorse for decisions you did take. I've done a lot of reflection about my decisions over the years and realised that I would take certain decisions differently in line with how my values have developed and how my experience has changed. Regardless, I wasn't that person at the time, and despite having made numerous decisions that had less than ideal outcomes, I would make almost all of these decisions again in the exact same situation because in that moment I was convinced it was my best option.

To learn and develop this skill of confident decision-making, focus on the process, and reflect on whether you executed your decision with confidence or if there was hesitation. If the latter is the case, try to identify the reasons, as you might have lacked clarity in key elements that are important to your own decision-making process. Confidence in decision-making is also connected with accepting that we can't go back and decide differently because we'll never be in the exact same situation again. The next time we're faced with a similar choice, we might be a different person, in a different context and situation, all of which make it a different decision. We hardly ever know what lies on the other side of a decision, so confidence is found in what you can influence. The key to confident decision-making lies in looking at the process, meaning the way the decision is deliberated, how the choices are developed, and which criteria are finally taken into consideration. All of these elements are adaptable to who takes the decision and in which context.

In addition, when filling the role of decision-maker in a crisis, we must accept that we'll make choices that have negative consequences and unintended outcomes, which might make the situation worse instead of improving it. It's important to remember that we never make decisions in a void, where only our decision is relevant and important. The complexity of the system makes results difficult to foresee, so the process of building confidence beforehand is very important. The outcomes might not always be what we hoped for, and the situation might become even more challenging, but if it's possible to explain the reasoning and process that led to the decision, our conviction and confidence will increase. Lastly, whether it's leadership, decision-making, or something entirely different, I've never been a fan of judging things as right or wrong. I can state my opinion on whether I personally agree, but I've learned not to allow myself to judge or qualify the decisions of others, as their realities and reasoning might differ from my own. Particularly in a crisis, I strongly advise staying away from qualifications because they are mostly made from a position that can't be related to. This determination is dependent on the eye of the beholder, the people concerned, and ultimately by the one making the decision.

THE POWER OF INTUITION

As you've gathered by now, I worked in many conflict zones around the world, and I remember each one of them clearly. As mentioned before, during my time in Afghanistan, some days, I would leave the house with the feeling that something was different. It was a small itch – a hunch somewhere deep inside – so subtle that it might as well have gone unnoticed, but nevertheless a regular occurrence I eventually realised it often coincided with days of security incidents. The more I paid attention to this so-called sixth sense, the more I understood its frequency meant there was more to this than simple coincidence and a random feeling. I also started to realise that this can be a real asset and began to work on exploring what we commonly label a "gut feeling."

However, this isn't just a feeling but more a reaction to an unknown trigger, where the hardest step in developing the skill of exploring your triggers is to become aware of your intuition and subconscious responses. The aim mustn't be to immediately identify the reason that triggers your intuitive response but to acknowledge and learn the signs our body gives out because they're not the same in everyone. It's about sharpening your senses and becoming more open to your body's reactions to situations or choices that you're facing. Once your awareness has increased, you will realise that your gut feeling is quite active and gives its "opinion" on way more of your potential decisions than you initially thought, at which point you're in good contact with your intuition. You might also reflect on and discover reasons why you react subconsciously by identifying what the trigger was in certain situations. This contributes to your increased self-awareness, self-clarification, and finding potentially hidden solutions to how you can deal with the present or future circumstances.

I'm not proposing that every decision should be purely based on our intuition because – as with many of our other cognitive processes – it's subject to bias and heavily influenced by our previous experiences. However, regularly exploring our subconscious signals will make it easier for us to realise our biases and contribute to learning and improving our decision-making. Like wine, intuition ages well into tacit knowledge; the type of knowledge we can't always put into words. The more experiences we make, the more comparisons our subconscious has available for its quick assessment of a situation, a context, or a decision and the more foundation can be found for it. With age comes an increasing appreciation for the fact that the gut feeling has its value; however, the choice is still for a person to make.

DEALING WITH DILEMMA DECISIONS

Back in the car in eastern DRC, the debate continued between Jean, who became increasingly nervous, and the policeman, who became increasingly insistent, so I decided that I needed to get back into the situation and intervene in a different way. I asked Jean to inform the policeman that I was the one he needed to address and that Jean was translating from then on. Re-entering the communication and redirecting attention allowed me to regroup. Jean then helped translate there had been a misinterpretation and we would not drive to headquarters because we were only visitors and did not work there. I also pointed out that we were willing to pay a reasonable fine for the offence, but not the amount that was asked. I informed him that if we couldn't agree on this we would happily drive to the police station to talk to his supervisor and enquire about reasonable payment. The situation turned into a negotiation, and in the end, we paid a small fine, which he proceeded to pocket, and we agreed to drop the policeman back at the station.

Dilemmas are inherent to every single crisis. Should you take an alleged human trafficker into a refugee camp because only he can make your humanitarian operation happen? Which way to send a car full of your staff that's stuck between a known kidnapping zone in one direction and active crossfire in the other? Should you share with your employer information that you know would be of huge advantage to them but was given to you in confidence? When faced

146

with a critical situation, there are almost always moments when we must decide, knowing that none of the options will lead to a desirable outcome and that whichever choice we make will have negative impacts. Dilemmas are common and a special kind of decision that doesn't create confidence for stakeholders in their own choice and option.

There are different models that support decision-making in dilemma situations, and often, the discourse focuses on ethics and moral considerations. The challenge with dilemmas is that seemingly everything is a wrong choice because no matter what, something and/or someone will be affected negatively. But like other terms, morals and ethics don't have a common interpretation, so we must ask ourselves whether it's difficult for us to make a choice because of our own morals and ethics or because of what we think to be the general ethics and morals around the issue or situation. While the latter can be an influential factor for what the final decision could be, it might not necessarily contribute to having confidence and owning the decision. Giving our own value and moral system priority, on the other hand, might not be popular but is likely to increase our personal confidence in our decision.

From my experience, the most effective way to handle this is to change the perspective and reframe the situation. If every option is an equally bad one, then each of them is also equally good. This slight change of mindset helped me to approach dilemma decisions differently. Then it is all about connecting with your intuition, which shows you where your confidence is hiding, about the most positive option. Another important element is acceptance. After accepting that we will face negative consequences, we can reflect on which ones we would rather deal with and consequently choose the option that most likely leads to them. This way, we shift our focus from the decision

147

to dealing with the negative side-effects of it. We must, however, be aware of the assumption trap when it comes to outcomes. Overall, there is no general answer to a dilemma decision, and ultimately these are choices where I recommend getting perspectives and a debrief afterwards; talk through how you got to the choice and what factors were taken into consideration. This allows you to get to know your own dilemma navigator and become safer and more confident in your decisions in potential future situations.

The story I shared from the DRC is illustrative of dilemmas being more than just moral and ethical in nature. There are often legal, practical, or systemic implications to consider. In that example, it quickly became clear that the policeman's interest was personal financial gain by using his authority, and I decided to reprioritise in terms of which criteria I used for my intervention. I didn't follow my moral compass here. Rather, I looked at the implications for us as individuals and the organisation we represented. I followed my own intuition and aimed for everyone to save face by opting not to address all the lines we had crossed, which led to our paying a fee that disappeared into the policeman's pocket. This might be looked upon as morally wrong by some, as illegal by others, and unethical by many more. Nevertheless, I'm confident that this decision was the one to take there and then, as it got us out of the situation safely and without any further trouble, and it's a decision I would make again.

KEY TAKE-AWAYS

▶ Decisions have two parts, the choice and the implementation, and are only complete if both are fulfilled. Therefore, consider whether you own the decision, including your leverage for implementation.

▶ The decision-making process should result in a decision made with confidence and conviction, despite any outcome. Do not judge your decisions based on the outcome because it's always an unknown variable.

▶ Focusing on possible results is based on assumptions and can mislead us throughout the decision-making process. Focus on the process and criteria instead.

▶ Learn how to use your intuition in an effective way. Explore your gut feeling and find ways to understand its origin. What is hidden beyond it is often-crucial knowledge and value-based reactions.

▶ Dilemmas follow the same logic as every other decision. To avoid getting distracted by the negative outcomes try to reframe the options as equally good. Choices become slightly easier with a positive mental frame around them. Decide on the criteria for decision-making before you know the topic.

THE AFTERMATH

Crises are often talked about as having a beginning and an end, but in reality, they're fluid time periods. I like to refer to crises as peaks in an ongoing process like the curves of a heartbeat during an ECG. Rather than abruptly ending, crises phase out and transition back into the more constant change process.

Crisis management is prone to post-peak energy loss. When the worst for us is over, the adrenalin levels drop, and we need to relax and take a break. This is dangerous, as the context around us doesn't stop evolving. There are learning opportunities, and we might fall back into a difficult situation before we know it. It's essential to keep in mind that having dealt with a crisis doesn't mean that there won't be any more difficult decisions to make.

Crises always result in a significant change of the context and system that was affected by it. This, consequently, requires us to deal with the changes that resulted from our decisions and to grow, nurture, and manifest the new system. It's key not to lose focus, follow through with what was decided, and the course that was taken during the difficult times. The danger with letting too much time pass is that, yet again, we end up a step behind and all the hard work of reinvention during difficult times is prone to getting lost.

That said, it's equally key to attend to the human side, especially after critical periods. I have repeatedly pretended that it's possible to just move on after a short break, and this was never a good idea. On the contrary, it cost me dearly at one point, when my body decided to take over and stop me. I hit a wall. A thorough reflection, a full debriefing, and an honest look in the mirror are essential after having worked through a crisis. It makes us stronger, shows us our resilience and our limitations, and helps us make sense of many things that might have rushed by during the challenging period.

The biggest mistake we can make is focusing only on supporting others because they seem to need the assistance and self-care can wait. Know this, however: it cannot wait. Like on a plane, it's about putting on your own oxygen mask first.

Crises are peaks, and we can work on avoiding them, but it's not always easy in today's fast-paced world as confronted with ever-changing dynamics. I've learned to focus on what I can readily control because there will always be critical situations to manage, and readiness helps us to approach them without the extreme peaks of emotions, pressure, and consequences but as a natural way to develop. We must make decisions constantly, and some weigh more than others, but starting with ourselves and our own skills and habits, we can build our own compass to help manage the constant uncertainty swirling around us and navigate beyond crises.

FINAL THOUGHTS

So, what can we conclude from all of this?

Let's demystify the term crisis. We must accept crises as natural, unavoidable, and necessary steps on our journey – and something we will face plenty of throughout our lives. Ironically, while we all use the word, crisis remains an individual mental frame, meaning that we are giving it sense and meaning based on our own experience. This interpretation also determines how we react to it. At their core, however, all crises require us to make decisions about significant changes. Sadly, the definition has shifted into overwhelmingly negative territory, while it was initially neutral. In many situations, we adopt a crisis narrative without reflecting on what the crisis is actually about and whether it concerns us. We quickly jump on a crisis narrative without considering the potential consequences. However, we don't even have to call a situation a crisis in most cases. Avoiding branding a context a crisis can be a decisive advantage because it doesn't provoke unwanted emotional reactions, thereby potentially hampering the ability to respond.

Let's stop underestimating ourselves. Crises are all about people. We are born with natural abilities to adapt and reinvent ourselves during crises and find ways through the most challenging periods (or appear to be so). We frequently give in to the temptation to attribute responsibility to the changing context, thus undermining our leverage and options. And there is always another option. Desperation makes us creative and inventive, though we don't have to be cornered to unleash this potential. We have all the skills it takes, and through applying simple habits, we can create a fundamental readiness for the unknown we are yet to encounter.

Let's prepare ourselves differently. Trying to foresee the dimensions of a potential crisis has proven ineffective and inaccurate. Despite our best efforts, we can never really predict how it will evolve and change. Given modernity's complexity, such attempts are at best assumptions, and it's time to think differently. Instead of wasting endless resources on trying to predict a future situation that is yet unknown, we have all the possibilities to get ready to avoid disruption for when it finally occurs. When confronted with what seems to be an impossibly complex context, these habits will pay off and allow us to make sense of the situation, defining our problem. They will enable us to reinvent our resources to find creative solutions and reclaim ownership of the outcome.

Let's reconnect. I've had the privilege to observe the magic of resilience in the most unlikely places, and while it lies in each of us, it's even more powerful when we remember our interconnectedness. Fighting crises alone or from an individual perspective makes us vulnerable and ultimately costs more than we might achieve. We are incredibly resourceful, all of us alone, but coming together is the most effective way to face any crisis.

Let's continue to learn. Looking back at many years of being surrounded by daily crises didn't provide me with all the answers for what to do when the next one comes. We all have limitations, though these should be motivations to learn and discover new ways. Like everything around us, we constantly develop and learn, though we're not always aware of it because most of these processes are invisible. Making explicit what we learned can make all the difference in a challenging situation. It's in our own hands to be ready when the next crisis comes, regardless of its shape and form.

Let's become adventurers and explorers. Every crisis is a pathway into undiscovered territory. If we're ready, we can turn those situations into the chance to find our ways and explore what's waiting in what we so generally label the unknown. The beauty of the unknown is that it's nothing but the future. And the future is built on our decisions. Our ideas combined with our resources, innate resilience, and a healthy dash of curious determination, are all we need to be perfectly equipped to navigate beyond any crisis.

TOOLBOX

CRISIS PROFILING

A fun way to do this is through what I call crisis profiling. Crisis profiling is inspired by criminal profiling and plays on the idea of dissecting the behaviour and profile of a crisis by developing a persona. It's recommended that you do this with other people to ensure different perspectives. These people can be connected or affected by the crisis, but it's also advantageous to have people who aren't connected to the crisis at all. Imagine you're about to meet this person for a blind date. Make sure you think of the crisis when you follow the steps below.

Method:
• Draw a picture of a person and give them a name.
• Create a character and describe their different characteristics.
• Think about the person's network and connections.
• Describe your relationship with the person.
• Identify assumptions and where you need more information.

STOP, SHARE, EXPLORE, REFRAME

This is an effective exercise to capture emotional responses. It can be done at any moment or when the situation has changed significantly.

Method:
• Stop an activity without any prior announcement.
• Do a round, asking how the situation makes the people feel and/or what it triggers in them.

- After collecting said information, explore some of the emotions collectively in an appreciative dialogue and take note of the reasons for the reactions.
- Reframe the triggers into potential solutions.

Depending on the cohesiveness of the team and the severity of the situation, this can be done openly or in written form and then read out anonymously. It can be followed by a short appreciative dialogue about the things mentioned, at which point it's also made clear that all emotions are allowed. I repeat this and/or other exercises regularly over the course of the crisis management session, as internal dynamics add their share of emotional triggers.

TO-DO LIST STOCK MARKET

One of the most subtle ways to find out hidden resources and make your team aware of who has them is to put your to-do list on the table. This way you can attribute specific – and sometimes hidden – talents to team members. This activity has the nice side effect that it brings the team together through sharing vulnerability and collectively working on the tasks.

Method:
- Share your to-do list with your team and ask them to share theirs.
- Highlight tasks that are difficult for you to complete or that you struggle with.
- Ask if team members can help or take over tasks.
- Repeat this process for all team members.

DECONSTRUCTING MENTAL MODELS

This exercise helps to practice the openness for alternative solutions. It feeds into fostering the MacGyver mindset and helps to create new ideas. Optionally, it can be carried out under time pressure to increase mental mind shift abilities.

Method:
- Identify a resource and specify it as much as possible.
- Outline all the ways you can use this resource.
- Find alternative and unusual ways to make use of this resource.

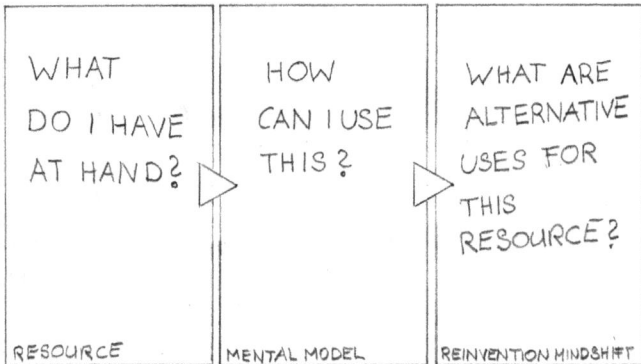

```
WHAT            HOW             WHAT ARE
DO I HAVE       CAN I USE       ALTERNATIVE
AT HAND?   ▷    THIS?      ▷    USES FOR
                                THIS
                                RESOURCE?

RESOURCE        MENTAL MODEL    REINVENTION MINDSHIFT
```

CREATIVE ALTERNATIVE COMPETITION

This wonderful short exercise that's often used in conflict resolution workshops can be a great way to practice the mind shift in a playful manner. It not only stimulates creativity, but participants are also encouraged to break down mental models collectively.

Method:
- Form small teams of 3–4 people.
- Take any object.

160

- Give the instruction to identify as many ways as possible for how this object can be used . . .
    - so more than one person can benefit from it
    - in other sectors
    - as a toy
    - and so on . . . you can get creative with categorisations here
- Collect all the answers and emphasise the overall number in addition to congratulating the winners.

TEAM RESOURCE DISCOVERY QUIZ

This is a playful way to discover the varying resources of team members. These are just sample questions, and you can work with any other questions you deem fitting. To get the answers to these questions, it might require the right moment, patience, and time for teams to grow and develop, as this is also very much dependent on multi-party cohesion. It is, however, worth exploring some of them because everything that you discover isn't only a resource, but it also allows colleagues to get to know each other better, thus strengthening their sense of togetherness.

Method:
Open or close every meeting with one of the questions below, and let team members answer secretly.

- Which languages does each team member speak and to what degree?
- Where have they travelled or lived? Have they been abroad?
- Have any of my team members worked in a different sector/ profession or does anyone have any training or formal education they aren't presently using?
- Has anyone written a book or any other publication?

- Do any of my team members have any licenses/qualifications? If so, which ones?
- What potentially important connections do my team members have?

RESOURCE GUARDIANS

If you have particularly valuable resources that you have to be careful with, assign a guardian within your team to keep an eye on how this asset is maintained, recharged, and/or used.

LEARNING RELAY BATON

Make mentioning and observation of learnings a shared responsibility by assigning a figurative or physical relay baton that's passed amongst your team members and that carries the responsibility to observe and capture insights on how the team learns. This way, you include everyone and ensure that it's a regular topic. You could carry out a gamified version where the baton-holder mustn't be discovered.

SUCCESS SESSION

Have a regular specific meeting where you only name, explore, and talk about what you do and did extremely well. Not all successes are results or achievements, so make sure to throw practices and habits into the mix as well. The meeting can be facilitated in different ways to ensure that everyone participates. The results should be recorded.

SUCCESS BOWL

Place a bowl in your office or home, and make sure its location is prominent. Ask people to write a note and put it in the bowl whenever they've achieved something. This way, you not only collect successes but motivate people to share and collect them by seeing how the bowl fills up. The successes can be shared during a meeting, at the end of a month, or any other time.

SO WHAT?

This learning exercise helps you ensure that insights, conclusions, and results are clear and transferrable into actions. It can be applied in different formats, such as workshops, learning events, or meetings, to ensure collective ownership.

Method:
- Decide on an object or a signal that people can use when they want to raise a "so what?"
- Throughout the session, people can use the items to signal when they're not clear on particular information/data or how to apply what was said.
- When a "so what?" item is raised, do not dismiss it but work on specifying how and why this insight is useful and how it can be practically applied.

DECISION NAVIGATOR

So how to work with all of this as a helpful guiding framework? Bringing together my experience and observations accumulated over the last years, I created the Decision Navigator, a dynamic five-step process to approaching crisis management. These elements help to create a structure for navigating decision-making while remaining adaptable through regular reassessment, and scalable with the complexity of the problem. I recommend working with a facilitator role to keep control over the process and not mix mandates.

STEP 1: RESOURCE INVENTORY

This first step is inspired by both MacGyver and the resourcefulness of my mother's cooking skills. She is the master of improvisation and making use of whatever is in the fridge thanks to a regular resource inventory. Even more than in cooking, this is important when facing a critical situation. Resources play a key role in making confident decisions and are the base for your journey to reinvention in a crisis.

Method
These steps won't provide you with a complete list, but they give you a foundation for how you can do a quick resource inventory. While the questions below might not all seem relevant, I highly recommend going through each of them in the correct order, as they're specifically designed and tested to help you uncover blind spots.

1. What are our existing resources?
Note: Use the prompts in the resource chapter and work beyond visible resources.

2. Which resources are currently in use, and which are not?

Note: If the answer is all or most of them are in use, you might have blind spots, as no organisation uses all of their resources at any given point in time.

3. What resources would we like to have, want, or need?

Note: Make this independent of a specific context and focus on the gaps in existing resources.

4. Which of our desired resources do we have access to?

Note: The ones you do not have access to can be dismissed immediately, so they don't interfere with any potential plan.

Do the resource inventory as a separate exercise, which isn't related to a situation such as a present crisis or a specific problem. Don't start with a current context or issue.

The reason for this is that any given context will influence your perception, and you'll naturally focus on the resources that you have traditionally worked in a comparable situation.

Make sure you document the results carefully to be able to use them in later steps.

STEP 2: ZOOM OUT – SYSTEMIC CRISIS PROFILING

While I keep emphasising that it's essential to focus on the actual problem at hand and consequently one's own scope of influence, the first step is to understand the situation and context in which the crisis happens. Every crisis is primarily a label for a period where decisions are unavoidable. Each has its profile, which needs to be analysed using a systemic point of view before being able to identify how it relates to your situation. Step two of the Decision Navigator is zooming out so you can profile your crisis. The five points below make for the core elements of systemic crisis profiling. Feel free to add and explore different aspects if you see them as relevant, but make sure all perspectives are acknowledged and taken into consideration. Avoid working in terms of "right" or "wrong," and be sure to maintain an explorative mindset. The basic idea of zooming out is to establish a common understanding within your team and organisation of the overall circumstances. The process thrives on different perspectives and viewpoints, so I recommend making this a group exercise.

1. Share your individual perceptions and descriptions of the situation.

If the wider context feels too general for your situation, choose a focus and start to describe your perception. The aim isn't to discuss the problems but the contexts around them.

2. Identify dynamics and elements of the system.

This can seem rather advanced for someone who hasn't worked with systems thinking before, but it's primarily about identifying how your context works. This means knowing which elements are connected, how to the influence each other, and how this affects the situation in return. Systems are dynamic, and it's important to identify interconnections and relationships.

3. Who are key stakeholders and actors?

I purposefully don't speak only of stakeholders because actors are equally important. The distinction is simply that stakeholders have the power to make decisions that affect the system on a large scale and can change the balance, while actors are less powerful and more frequently on the receiving end. Here, it's essential to look at the different interests at play, as they might affect the behaviour of the situation. This is key information for your own crisis management. One of the things most easily forgotten is to control whether we are part of the system and how this affects us. If the analysed situation does not directly concern you, large scale crisis management might not be needed. If it does, however, it's important to understand how. Therefore, look at where you are in the system and how you got there.

4.What are our leverage points?

Remember that systems are dynamic, and they tend to develop lives of their own as a means to self-perpetuate. In crises, you might want to aim to completely change a system, which is why it's important to understand how far your scope of influence goes. With this final question, you can analyse your actual scope of influence within the system. This way, you assess what can change and how far your power reaches. Leverage points don't necessarily mean that you can immediately start working on them, so you must not make the mistake of assuming you can create change easily, as you might still need to identify your barriers and problems and develop solutions for them.

I recommend that you repeat this exercise regularly and independently of the other steps of the Decision Navigator method because it will ensure you frequently establish a common understanding of the situation and identify opportunities, blind spots, and traps.

STEP 3: ZOOM IN – PROBLEM DEFINITION

Following a combined understanding of the crisis at hand and the deconstruction of its elements, it's important to find out what the actual problems for you, your team, and your organisation are. Too many companies are unable to define their actual problems and lose themselves in focusing on situations that aren't within their scope of influence. Throughout the COVID-19 pandemic, we often heard what to do about travel restrictions while the more accurate question might have been, "How can we continue to run our business despite the travel restrictions?" This is due to an overflow of information (which needs to be analysed and condensed) and a lack of ability to re-focus on our own scope of influence. Furthermore – and this is one of the most important competencies to have in a crisis – these organisations struggle to prioritise which problem to focus on solving first. Start by making a list of all the problems that come to mind, and then apply the following questions to prioritise and define:

1. What is the most urgent problem to solve?

Find ways to prioritise problems. Also, I recommend working with different perspectives and a clear procedure for how to rank them. Once all problems are ranked, you can begin working on them. Given that the system is dynamic, this list is fluid, the ranking will change, and new problems will appear or disappear.

2. What makes this a problem for us?

Double-check if this is an actual problem for your organisation. In many cases, this step reveals that it's difficult to say why this is a problem, which naturally leads to refining how it's formulated or being able to dismiss it.

3. What other actors and stakeholders have an interest in this?

In this step, it's important to identify who else is faces this problem and has an interest in it to be solved or not. List the actors and their interest in the problem. Include their influence over the situation.

4. How can we own the problem?

This step is about reframing the problem so it's within your ownership. By making the problem precise, it's easier to work out solutions at a later stage. The most effective way is to formulate a problem question from your own perspective, as outlined in the introduction to this segment. Make a final check to determine whether this problem lies within your scope of influence and, if so, to what degree. If you don't fully own the problem, review its formulation once again. Alternatively, you can decide to continue working with it regardless or return to the problem list.

STEP 4: CHOICE SPECTRUM EXPANSION

Use this step to expand your spectrum of options and solutions beyond what is naturally presented by the context and crisis, thereby expanding your room for manoeuvre. When you create your own options, the feeling of ownership returns because you feel like you can act and get ahead of the situation. It is highly recommended that that the final decision-makers are not part of this process to avoid any potential bias. Creativity is key during this step, and any method can be applied to complete the following:

1. What are our ideas?

Use your resource inventory to map ideas for how to solve your priority problem. Start by mapping these out. It's essential to work with realism here and that the choices are actionable and simple to understand. Furthermore, it's important that they are directly based on the resources available to you and thus can be realised. Be creative, and don't dismiss ideas at this stage. Also, consider the natural solutions that each problem is presented with. Based on this, you can already assess the existing space of influence.

2. What are our preferred ideas?

Select the top five ideas from the spectrum to take forward in the process. Agree beforehand on the criteria and format for how this ranking is done. Allow for differing perspectives and be clear on your reasoning.

3. What are the costs and effort of each idea?

As a first criterion, discuss how much effort and cost each of these ideas will entail. Give special consideration to resources that are limited in stock.

4. Do we have leverage over the ideas?

This step helps you to assess whether you have the autonomy and ability to realise each of these ideas. If not, you might want to consider dismissing the idea.

5. What are the top three options?

In the final step of this segment you transform your ideas into actual options by selecting the top three ideas based on the additional information from the previous steps. These present the final choices that the decision-makers are presented with.

STEP 5: CONFIDENT DECISION-MAKING

The preceding four phases lay the groundwork for a confident decision. Next is finding a concluding process for how to come to a final choice. This step is a flexible one, as it depends on the organisation, team, or person making the decisions, though I strongly recommend not being involved in the previous steps leading up to this point if you're the decision-maker. Let the team present the outcomes and some recommendations for what they think the decision-making process should look like, and then make your decision. The advantage of this separation is that you aren't involved in developing solutions, which enables you to be less biased. This way, you can listen to your intuition and explore your reactions to the options presented in a clearer and more open-minded way. By the team putting forward a whole pitch, including the results of all four steps, you receive a comprehensive picture and, if you desire, a recommendation as well. With this process, you share responsibility for finding solutions, thereby creating inclusion and collective ownership. This requires an open mindset and the ability to let go of controlling the whole process while the crisis is being managed and trusting the team that's been tasked with the Decision Navigator, which will serve all parties well when the decisions are being implemented. Consult with your team about the preferred way for decisions to be made, and ensure you explain once a decision is made without justifying your choice.

Optional steps for this phase:

1. What is the decision-making process going to look like?

This step is underestimated in its importance. Clarity on the decision-making process is essential in any phase of the crisis. It is essential clarify and align expectations and understanding.

2. What are the potential outcomes of each of the choices?

This is about making assumptions explicit and discuss the anticipated scenario.

3. How are we dealing with unexpected outcomes?

This question should help to get mentally ready for an unexpected outcome. Focus on the process for how you would react in the discussion.

4. What are the remaining doubts?

Answering this question will help you identify potential insecurities around the choices and explore options to eliminate them and assess your conviction levels for each choice.

The Decision Navigator process can be repeated for different problems and in shorter and more extensive forms. The idea isn't only to create a structured approach to managing crisis but one that provides the necessary flexibility, serves as an anchor, and documents how decisions were made.

Sources:

Goshi, Anisa (2021). The Art of Resilience. TEDxCIFE.

Klein, Gary (2009). Streetlights and Shadows: Searching for the Key to Adaptive Decision Making. MIT Press, Cambridge, Massachusetts.

Schulz von Thun, Friedemann (2010). Störungen und Klärungen: Allgemeine Psychologie der Kommunikation, Rowohlt Taschenbuch Verlag, Hamburg.

Sharot, Tali (2018). Why Stressed Minds Are Better at Processing Things, https://www.bbc.com/future/article/20180613-why-stressed-minds-are-better-at-processing-things

Taleb, Nassim Nicholas (2007). The Black Swan: The Impact of the Highly Improbable, Random House, New York.

Thomas Lahnthaler is an experienced international crisis leader, mediator, facilitator, and speaker and the founder and CEO of The Crisis Compass. He has worked in crisis and conflict zones around the world over two decades and 30 countries responding to some of the most complex emergencies of our time. A strong advocate for learning across sectors, Thomas advises and teaches crisis management to leaders, teams, and organisations globally.

www.ingramcontent.com/pod-product-compliance
Lightning Source LLC
Chambersburg PA
CBHW071553200326
41519CB00021BB/6725